The Buck Stops Here

Claudia Harris

TH E BUCK STOPS HERE

This book is written to provide information and motivation to readers. Its purpose is not to render any type of psychological, legal, or professional advice of any kind. The content is the sole opinion and expression of the author, and not necessarily that of the publisher.

Copyright © 2019 by Claudia Harris

All rights reserved. No part of this book may be reproduced, transmitted, or distributed in any form by any means, including, but not limited to, recording, photocopying, or taking screenshots of parts of the book, without prior written permission from the author or the publisher. Brief quotations for noncommercial purposes, such as book reviews, permitted by Fair Use of the U.S. Copyright Law, are allowed without written permissions, as long as such quotations do not cause damage to the book's commercial value. For permissions, write to the publisher, whose address is stated below.

Printed in the United States of America.

ISBN   978-1-64552-097-9   (Paperback)
ISBN   978-1-64552-098-6   (Digital)

Lettra Press books may be ordered through booksellers or by contacting:

Lettra Press LLC
18229 E 52nd Ave.
Denver City, CO 80249
1 303 586 1431 | info@lettrapress.com
www.lettrapress.com

Dedicated to My Brother Will and his lovely wife
And to my children and grandchildren

This book is written with respect to all religions,
peoples, and persuasions.

CONTENTS

Preface ix

1 — Religion Today 1
2 — Women in the Ministry 9
3 — God's Prosperity 14
4 — The Church 26
5 — Love 56
6 — Death 63

Author Biography 73

PREFACE

I have been in Christ a lifetime. God has been preparing me for this work for approximately fifty-five years. The soul is like gold. Gold has to be purified, and purification comes from heat—trials and suffering. Gold is worthless unless the dross has been removed; likewise, the soul, or self, has to die. Isaiah 48:10 says, "Behold, I have refined thee but not with silver; I have chosen thee in the furnace of affliction." I was in God's furnace of affliction for many years, but I was never alone. God was with me. He was preparing me as a vessel to be used for service. The Holy Spirit does the work, but he has to have a body to work through. A beautiful instrument is worthless without a player. And, regardless of the beauty or value of the instrument, the instrument is never praised; all praise and honor go to the individual who skillfully plays it.

I married at the age of twenty-one, and that was the beginning of my furnace. I had been raised in a sheltered environment and had no experience of life. In fact, my view of life at that age was one got married and lived happily ever after—the fairy-tale marriage. I was very naive. My marriage, however, ended in divorce, and that was devastating for me. Years ago, divorce was taboo, and in some churches that I visited people would say, "God is not with you, because you are divorced." Being a single working mom was not easy, but God had other plans for my life, and I truly needed that experience for growth and maturity.

At times I felt that I just couldn't make it any further, but God would give me just enough hope and strength to keep going day by day. My family doctor at that time suggested that I take nerve pills and wrote a prescription. I took them for a few days, but I told myself that I was not going to go through life depending on a pill. While out for a walk one day, I threw that bottle of pills into a wooded area, and that was the end of the nerve pills. It was not easy, but I was determined to hold on to God's unchanging hand. There were times when I was just hanging on emotionally to a song, but the song would get me through the day and give me the strength that I needed to face the next day. The song "I Must Tell Jesus All of My Trials" was medicine for me—spiritual food! The testimonies that former saints have left behind in the form of hymns are consoling. I was also strengthened and consoled by many inspirational poems, which I sometimes passed on to others. Perfect faith is a process. It takes time—years. The apostle Peter thought that he was strong enough to follow Jesus to the cross, but Jesus in his infinite wisdom knew that Peter would deny him—the spirit or mind to follow may be strong, but the flesh is weak. God's love draws people out of bad situations. Some of the things that I have cried about in my life, I laugh about today. You just have to hang in there and never give up.

Many of you have heard the saying "out of the frying pan and into the fire." Well, I went from God's furnace to the cross—crucified! If you are a true follower of Christ, that is the process. However, the cross is significant. Remember, when Jesus was on the cross, he endured great pain and suffering, but he was also high and lifted up. Enemies and friends were there to watch, but putting Jesus on the cross was Satan's mistake! John 12:32 says, "I, if I be lifted up from the earth, will draw all men unto me."

Symbolically, there is pain and suffering in our individual crucifixions, but our stories do not end there. When all the persecutors and foes have counted you out, when people cease to call and visit, and when no one wants to be around you, guess what: if God has ordained your suffering for divine purpose, to give you needed experience, when everyone, even you, thinks that life is over for you, God will send his angel to roll the stone away, and you will rise! Psalm 40:1–3 says, "I waited patiently for the Lord; and he inclined unto me, and heard my cry. He brought me up also out of a horrible pit, out of the miry clay, and set my feet upon a rock, and established my goings. And he hath put a new song in my mouth, even praise unto our God. Many shall see it, and fear, and shall trust in the Lord."

I have risen in the form of books, books that God has given to me to write for him. Writing is the anointing that the Holy Spirit has placed on my life. The poem "Religion" in chapter 4, "The Church," is not of myself; it was given to me by the Holy Spirit. Writing was never on my agenda. When God revealed to me that he wanted me to write, he placed the individuals that I needed to accomplish this task in my path. For example, I never went out of my way to look for a publisher.

One day while traveling to Michigan, I casually mentioned to a woman on the bus that God wanted me to write a book. She said, "I knew that I was going to meet you when you stepped onto this bus." She told me that God was going to reveal the book in substance. "You should keep pen and paper with you at all times," she said. "His revelation will come only once in thought, and if you don't write it down, you won't remember it later." She also said that I should remember that it was not my book but the book that God had given me to write for him. Then, she prayed for me, God's angel.

A week or so later, while riding home from work on the bus, the poem "Religion" was revealed to me. I wrote the words down on scratch paper. After arriving home, I typed what I had written, and I had a poem—my first poem.

I am no longer on the cross. I have been resurrected. I have my BA (born again) and my PhD (praise him daily), and God has given me his peace that passes all understanding, joy in sorrow, and happiness. I am happy—happy with Jesus alone. God has been better to me than any husband, friend, or family member. God has let me have many, many rich experiences, including meeting many wonderful people and visiting many countries. However, he has never given me an abundance of material wealth. I've lived paycheck to paycheck for a lifetime, but the meal has never run out. As said in the story of Elijah, 1 Kings 17:14, "For thus saith the Lord God of Israel, The barrel of meal shall not waste, neither shall the cruse of oil fail." Money cannot buy the experiences that God has let me have in life. Let God choose your path!

I have also worked in the harvest—the vineyard of life—a lifetime. Proverbs 11:30 says, "And he that winneth souls is wise." I prefer walking and using public transportation, which affords me the opportunity to meet many people. In local travel, to save on hotel costs, I have sat on benches with homeless people, drug addicts, prostitutes, and disenfranchised individuals and witnessed--wonderful opportunities! To the homeless, the beggars, the lonely, and the disenfranchised, Jesus is not always in the fine car and big house with an important title to his name. Jesus is walking right beside you! He loves and cares for you, and if your heart and mind are open to receive him as Lord and savior, he will come in and sup with you!

In Despair
When we are despondent, downhearted, and sad
Because of the things we need and do not have,
Help us to remember, dear Lord, that in your Word you said,
If we put you first, the things we need,
You will add!

> But seek ye first the kingdom of God, and his righteousness; and all these things shall be added to you.
>
> —Matthew 6:33

The essence of this book is that God has one church, one body of born-again believers—the body of Christ. Each chapter in this book covers topics that divide, and there are many ad-lib discussions within this book on various topics from a practical point of view. I am spontaneous, and God has a sense of humor. Note that references I make regarding conversations with others happened forty-plus years ago and that I knew the individuals in passing as opposed to personally.

> And we know that all things work together for good to them that love God, to them who are the called according to his purpose.
>
> —Romans 8:28

God's Hall of Fame

Many of the names in God's hall of fame
Will be unknown to the world
Because the Lord keeps his own records
And he knows his own!
The greats in his kingdom
Will be those great and small
Who have kept his Word
And have witnessed to all;
Those who have visited the sick,
Helped a brother in need;
Those who have loved everyone,
In spite of race, color, or creed;
Those who have not accredited themselves
For accomplishments and fame,
Realizing that all good and perfect gifts
Come from the Father and that all glory,
Honor, and praise,
Go to his great name.
But when we get to heaven,
There we will claim
All the rewards God has in store for us
In his hall of fame.

> And whosoever shall exalt himself shall be abased, and he that shall humble himself shall be exalted.
>
> —Matthew 23:12

1

Religion Today

I was raised in a religious environment. Religion was basically my life. Sunday was the Lord's day. And religion wasn't only for Sundays. Each week there was Bible study, a prayer meeting, choir rehearsals, usher board meetings, revivals, and more. My dad was a pastor, and I went with him to many of his preaching engagements at other churches. In other words, one could say that I practically lived in the church.

As an adult, after I left home, I was not always able to attend services at my home church, so I visited churches in the many different areas where I lived. Even when traveling, I would visit local churches. I have attended worship services in many churches. Church was my thing or my enjoyment. Now that I am spiritually mature and in the homestretch of life, I can clearly see the difference between religion and salvation. "And that from a child thou hast known the Holy Scriptures which are able to make thee wise unto salvation through faith which is in Christ Jesus" (2 Timothy 3:15).

Religion is blinding. Religion crucifies Jesus over and over again. Why? Because many want to interpret the scriptures according to their knowledge and understanding. The Bible is a divinely inspired book, unfolded by revelation. "For now we see through a glass darkly; but then face to face: now I know in part" (1 Corinthians 13:12).

The mystery of the Bible, the written Word, is slowly unfolding. The Gentiles (non-Jewish people) were included in the calling of Abraham, the father of faith—salvation by faith. "And the scripture, foreseeing that God would justify the heathen through faith, preached before the gospel unto Abraham saying, In thee shall all nations be blessed. So then they which be of faith are blessed with faithful Abraham" (Galatians 3:8–9). Genesis 12:3 says, "And in thee shall all of the families of the earth be blessed." However, the Gentiles were not brought in completely until after the death of Jesus. Under the law, one could become a Jew by accepting Jewish traditions. As said in the story of Esther and Mordecai, "And many of the people of the land became Jews" (Esther 8:17).

Paul, the apostle sent to the Gentiles, was very religious. He was a Pharisee and a teacher of the law, but he did not fully understand the scriptures. Moses prophesied the coming of Jesus. "This is that Moses, which said unto the children of Israel, A prophet shall the Lord your God raise up unto you of your Brethren, like unto me; him shall ye hear. This is he, that was in the church in the wilderness" (Acts 7:37–38). Before Paul's conversion, he was a great persecutor of the early church. He delivered Christians up to be imprisoned and killed based on his interpretation of the law—that is, the scriptures. He honestly did not understand, and for that reason he was spared. Acts 9:16 says, "I will shew him what great things he must suffer for my name's sake," and 1 Timothy 1:12–13 reads, "And I thank Christ Jesus our Lord, who hath enabled me, for that he counted me faithful, putting me in the ministry; Who was before a blasphemer, and a persecutor, and injurious: but I obtained mercy because I did it ignorantly in unbelief."

As a child, I was not allowed to wear shorts or pants, and this made it difficult for me at school, especially in gym class, where we were required to wear blue shorts and white shirts. My dad, who was deeply religious, refused to let me wear such clothing because of his interpretation of Deuteronomy 22:5: "The woman shall not wear that which pertaineth unto a man." There was no flexibility with him. Because of this religious teaching, I had difficulty accepting women in so-called men's attire, like pants and shorts. My dad did, however, make a "lady" out of me, and I am in Christ today because of him. In interpreting scriptures, one has to know the culture of that day. Back then, men wore skirts. Men wearing skirts is spoken of throughout the Old Testament. For example, King David cut off the skirt of Saul ("Then David arose, and cut off the skirt of Saul" [1 Samuel 24:4]). There are many different interpretations of scriptures, and that is why religion can be dangerous.

God delivered me from this teaching by sending me to McDonald's to work. I was unemployed, could not find a job in my field, and was broke. I was hired the same hot day that I applied. I was given a uniform—shirt and pants. I stood a few seconds in amazement and said silently, *God, you know that I don't wear pants.* However, I had a mortgage to pay and no money, so I had to accept the uniform. That was the day that God set me free from the teaching that women should not wear shorts and pants. I seldom wear skirts and dresses today. Pants are easier to maintain, comfortable, and affordable, costing two to four dollars at a thrift store. I sometimes reflect back on the cold, cold Michigan winters when I stood at freezing-cold bus stops in a dress. I am now trying to make up for lost time.

I was also taught that eating in the church was wrong because the Bible teaches in 1 Corinthians 11:34 that "if any man hunger, let him eat at home." My childhood church did not have a basement or fellowship hall, and I attended other churches with similar beliefs. After I relocated from my home church, God placed me under new leadership with a church that had fellowship Sundays with dinners downstairs. God revealed to me that he wanted me to fellowship with them. I am not trying, though, to make up for the fried-chicken dinners that I missed, because good health and healthful food are at the top of my agenda.

It would be wonderful, in my perspective, if we, as the body of Christ, could let some of the doctrine go and focus on saving our youth. We have lost a generation, perhaps because we as a collective body are not as wise as the world. Are we still living in the horse-and-buggy days? Buggies were good in their day, but the world has changed. People are now driving cars. The world knows how to draw and attract, and young people have much to offer. If we cannot draw them in as a collective body, we cannot teach. Regardless of what is taught, some young people are going to be contrarians. But if the youth are taught, the promise is that they will come back to their foundations, the teachings of the church. Without a foundation, they will have nothing to come back to. There are those who are going to do as they please regardless. Alcohol, drugs, illicit sex, abortions, and so on, have been around for decades. Some people were doing these things years before legalization. Ecclesiastes 1:9 says, "There is no new thing under the sun."

God's basic principles never change, but methods—the way we do things—do change. My mother used a washtub and scrub board and heated water on the stove, as we had no running hot water, and we heated the house with a coal heater. Today, we have automatic washing machines, furnaces, and so on. Iceboxes, washboards, milkmen, and icemen are all out of date. In fact, one can no longer buy parts for many old items. New technology is being developed daily. The world has changed, but what about the church? What about the body of Christ? Are we still singing, "Give me that old-time religion—it's good enough for me"? Old-time religion is not working today. Are we as a body sitting down and waiting for our youth to come in on their own? This may never happen! We have to somehow, with united effort, "bring them in—go to them," as the songs: "Bringing In The Sheaves and Bring Them In."

Young people (and older people as well) enjoy food, music, dances, movies, plays, and creative activities. We can't do weed to unite with young people, but perhaps we can find a way to teach godliness through Christian entertainment. We can draw them in and let them write their own plays and compose their own godly Christian music. My grandkids can easily remember all the words to a popular song, but they can't remember their spelling words. Perhaps one could create a hip-hop song, the kind of music that you can dance to, telling them how important it is to learn to spell.

Sometimes I get out in left field, but my vision is to shut it all down some Sunday mornings and go sing and preach at the park—to have a cookout and invite all and to play spiritual music that feeds and consoles, like "Amazing Grace," "It Is Well," and so on. From my experience in listening and being in the harvest, the first thing that I hear from people is who their pastor is and how I should come and join their church.

Excuse me, but as a whole, many are not coming. Invite them to come to Jesus for salvation! That is the message. Let God and his Word draw them in. The Holy Spirit will lead them when and after they receive Christ. The message is the invitation to discipleship. The true church has no walls—it is a spiritual house.

The Christian life is not easy. Acceptance of Jesus Christ is just the beginning. Being born again means exactly what it says—a new birth and a brand-new life. The rules change. Everything takes time, but one must walk in a new direction—this is the newness of life. God requires holiness. It will take a lifetime to get it together, but one must start the journey. The journey of a thousand miles begins with the first step.

I enjoy reading about the human body. The human heart—one muscle—is the most fascinating part of the body to me. According to a book that I read, the heart has thousands and thousands of different aspects and cannot be studied in full. It has to be studied in sections. Cardiologists study for approximately fourteen years and more. This one muscle is so fascinating that I have not been able to move on to the study of the other organs. I am stuck, and I have not yet even touched upon God's creation—the world and all that dwells therein. I can't get past the operations of the heart. I need help! Psalm 139:14 says, "For I am fearfully and wonderfully made: marvellous are thy works."

Similarly, is the body of Christ "stuck" and divided on certain topics, especially on the calling of women into the ministry? Many of us have not gotten past that discussion. However, we have the Bible. When a car gets stuck in deep snow and ice, it's sometimes impossible to get it out without a tow truck. Does God need to send a tow truck to get us past this discussion? God validates—not men and women.

There are many in the body of Christ who refuse to let musical instruments into worship. But Matthew 24:31 says, "And he shall send his angels with a great sound of a trumpet, and they shall gather together his elect from the four winds, from one end of heaven to the other." Will those who refuse to let musical instruments into worship also refuse to rise from the grave on that great getting-up morning because they don't believe God uses trumpets? That may not be a bad thing, because they probably would not enjoy heaven, because there are trumpets and harps there. Revelation 14:2 says, "And I heard the voice of harpers harping with their harps," and Psalm 98:6 says, "With trumpets and sound of cornets make a joyful noise before the Lord, the King." And that is the end of that discussion.

The apostle Paul was not shaken by those who preached Christ and were not sincere, like those who were "teaching things which they ought not, for filthy lucre's [money's] sake" (Titus 1:11). Philippians 1:15–18 reads, "Some indeed preach Christ even of envy and strife … The one preach Christ of contention, not sincerely … What then? … whether in pretence, or in truth, Christ is preached; and I therein do rejoice." First Corinthians 4:5 reads, "Therefore judge nothing before the time, until the Lord come, who both will bring to light the hidden things of darkness, and will make manifest the Counsels of the hearts."

Let it all go! There will be a judgment day. The Bible is our guide—our road map to heaven. The answer to all problems can be found in the Bible. One need only read and study it. The books of Psalms, Proverbs, and Ecclesiastes are easily understood and help with everyday living, providing commonsense knowledge and summarizing life in general. For example, Proverbs 25:17 provides the practical knowledge to "withdraw thou foot from thou neighbor's house: lest he be weary of thee and so hate thee." In other words, don't visit your neighbor every day, or he or she will get sick and tired of you.

Bible knowledge, beyond God's salvation plan, will not get one into heaven, and neither will a lack of Bible knowledge keep one out. Romans 10:9 reads, "That if thou shalt confess with thou mouth the Lord Jesus and shalt believe in thine heart that God hath raised Him from the dead, thou shalt be saved." The thief that was crucified with Jesus did not have Bible knowledge, was not baptized, and did not have the spiritual gift of tongues—he simply believed that Jesus was the Son of God and instantly received eternal life. "And he said unto Jesus, Lord, remember me when thou cometh into thy kingdom. And Jesus said unto him, verily, I say unto thee, today shalt thy be with me in Paradise" (Luke 23:42–43).

Bible knowledge is, however, a great asset to have. The swimming pool is more enjoyable when one knows how to swim. Knowing how to swim can save one's life. Also, visiting another country can only be enjoyed to the fullest when one can speak the language. There are many versions of the Bible. Personally, I have been led by the Holy Spirit to write using the old King James Version. Let the spirit of God lead you. A layman's Parallel Bible may be a great idea for you, as it can help you easily compare the different versions.

I can say this with assurance: none of us can know God in his fullness. He is too great! How can one know a mind that great? Humankind has been studying the heart for decades. What about God's great creation? I have a one-on-one relationship with Jesus. No one can make me doubt him. I know he lives. If someone puts his or her hand in fire, no one on earth will be able to convince that person that fire doesn't burn. God is my heavenly Father, and Jesus is my best friend. I can talk to him silently in my heart about everything—all my hurts and fears—and I know that he listens, cares, and is going to do what is best for me. I trust his decisions for my life. However, to know how God operates and what his thoughts are or how he created the world is beyond human knowledge. Ecclesiastes 3:11 reads, "He has made everything beautiful in his time: also he hath set the world in their heart, so that no man can find out the work that God maketh from the beginning to the end." Isaiah 55:8–9 says, "For my thoughts are not your thoughts, neither are your ways my ways, said the Lord. For as the heavens are higher than the earth, so are my ways higher than your ways, and my thoughts than your thoughts."

I am not the authority. It is your prerogative to disagree. Life is similar to a large pot of soup. We can all contribute something. You too can write a book and share your thoughts. It is midnight for the church—the fig tree has blossomed, a sign of the times. Religion sometimes complicates salvation. John 3:16 says, "For God so loved the world, that he gave his only begotten Son, that whosoever believeth in him, should not perish, but have everlasting life."

Claudia Harris

Oath

    We, the body of Christ—the head, mind, eyes, ears, mouth, tongue, neck, arms, elbows, wrists, hands, fingers, heart, legs, ankles, feet, invisible parts, and bones—do solemnly agree to lay aside our differences, to love one another, and to work together in Christian love so that we, as one body, can grow together as one body, in spite of denomination, color, national origin, tongue, or the like. We will remain in our proper places and let the Holy Spirit lead and guide us so that he may be able to present us as "a glorious church, not having spot or wrinkle, or any such thing; but that it should be holy and without blemish" (Ephesians 5:27).

    The body is dead!

2

Women in the Ministry

The calling of women into the ministry has not been totally accepted by all in the body of Christ and thus causes division. The apostle Paul was born under the law, and much of his teachings center around the role of women. In the culture of that day, women were limited. Some scriptures have made it somewhat difficult for women who are called to the ministry, such as 1 Timothy 2:11–12, which says, "Let the women learn in silence with all subjection. But I suffer a woman not to teach nor to usurp authority over the man."

God's master plan from the beginning has included all that the Holy Spirit is bringing in today, including Gentiles and women. Hebrews 4:3 says that "the works were finished from the foundation of the world." Galations 3:29: "And if ye be Christ's then are ye Abraham's seed, and heirs according to the promise." All that is unfolding is a manifestation of this finished work, and there is a lot more to be revealed. Ephesians 1:10 reads, "That in the dispensation of the fullness of times he might gather together in one all things in Christ." The book of Revelation is filled with mysteries—things to come. God has a timetable for events. In the fullness of time, Jesus came on the scene. In another dispensation of the fullness of time, the apostle Paul and the Gentiles were brought in. God is pouring out his spirit on all flesh, and women are being brought in according to God's timetable.

In the beginning, God created Eve as a companion and helpmate to Adam—they were of equal status. "It is not good that man should be alone; I will make him a help meet for him ... and they shall be one flesh" (Genesis 2:18, 2:24). Eve was then deceived by the serpent, and she influenced Adam to also eat of the fruit from the tree of good and evil. "And Adam was not deceived, but the woman being deceived was in the transgression" (1 Timothy 2:14). However, the command to not eat of the tree had been given to Adam, and because of Adam's disobedience, sin entered into the world. "For as in Adam all die" (1 Corinthians 15:22). Adam and Eve now knew the difference between good and evil, and the punishment for their disobedience was the curse of the law. "Unto the woman [God] said ... and thy desire shall be to thy husband, and he shall rule over thee" (Genesis 3:16). "And unto Adam he said ... In the sweat of thy face shalt thou eat bread" (Genesis 3:17, 3:19).

Women became subservient to their husbands. Women, as a whole, were no longer totally free. Adam died a spiritual death due to his broken fellowship with God, and through his disobedience, all died. Humans had to be redeemed back to God. God's redemption plan was designed from the beginning and began with the calling of Abraham-- salvation by faith.

It has taken years for women to achieve many of the rights and opportunities that they have today. Women have not been as privileged as men. Psychologically, many men, especially in the older generations, have difficulty accepting women in leadership roles and positions. To change one's way of thinking takes time. But today, many can see the hand of God in his callings and anointings. I have done a lot of research and studying of God's Word to try to get a deeper understanding of this and other issues.

The apostle Paul wrote in Titus 2:4–5 that women should be keepers of the home. With the high cost of living today, the majority of the women that I know are employed outside of the home. I have met very few who have been able to be stay-at-home wives and mothers. A path has to be cleared for some things to happen. In my day, the majority of the women in my community were housewives and did not hold outside jobs. The man was the breadwinner. In fact, many of the jobs that women hold today were held by men only and were not open to women at all. The culture has changed since biblical times, but the basic principles of God, like the Ten Commandments, never change.

Now that I am thoroughly rooted in Christ and have religiously studied the scriptures, I know from scripture that the calling of women was ordained from the beginning: "Christ has redeemed us from the curse of the law, being made a curse for us " (Galatians 3:13). God's plan is like a puzzle. We do not have the complete picture—God does. We individually and collectively have only parts of the puzzle; however, as the puzzle comes together, we get a glimpse of the picture. Each dispensation brings in something new. The book of Revelation is filled with mysteries yet to be fulfilled. Many of the signs of the times that were prophesied are being fulfilled—children killing their parents, global warming and weather changes, division in families, violence in the land, the return of the ungodly living of the days of Noah, and so on. Sixty years ago, these things were seldom heard of. Children as a whole respected authority. They were corrected according to God's way (I am referring to godly parenting—not abuse). Today, the law is on the side of the child. The world has totally changed—and not for the better.

The Israelites were sincerely waiting for the Messiah's coming, but when Jesus arrived on earth, they did not recognize him. They had the scriptures, but Jesus did not come according to their expectations and their interpretation of scriptures (John 7:40–43). Many did not believe that Jesus was the Son of God. His mother, Mary, was not married to Joseph, and so it appeared that Jesus had been born out of wedlock and to a poor family. Jesus also was not, according to earthly standards, highly educated: "We be not born of fornication; we have one Father, even God" (John 8:41); "How knoweth this man letters, having never learned?" (John 7:15)

God uses women! Jesus was subject to his mother and his father. Women followed Jesus to the cross: "And many women were there beholding afar off, which followed Jesus from Galilee, ministering unto him" (Matthew 27:55). The message that Jesus was risen was given to women. "And the angel answered and said unto the women, Fear not ye: for I know that ye seek Jesus, which was crucified. He is not here for he is risen … And go quickly and tell his disciples" (Mathew 28:5–7). Women were in the upper room with the disciples on the day of Pentecost: "These all continued with one accord in prayer and supplication, with the women" (Acts 1:14). And also on the day of Pentecost, Peter stood up and said, "This is that which was spoken by the [Old Testament] prophet Joel; And it shall come to pass in the last days, saith God, I will pour out of my Spirit upon all flesh: and your sons and your daughters shall prophesy" (Acts 2:16–17).

When God calls an individual, that is validation, no matter whether people accept or reject that calling. "But the anointing which ye have received of him abideth in you, and ye need not that any man teach you" (1 John 2:27). A flock (church) can have only one shepherd, though. The apostle Paul did not want to labor on someone else's turf: "Yea, so have I strived to preach the gospel, not where Christ was named, lest I should build upon another man's foundation" (Romans 15:20). Female preachers can find new turf. We are surrounded by opportunities to minister, individually and collectively. Do not waste time with dead works. Launch out into the deep. Those who truly love Jesus and are concerned with the path that many of our youth have taken know that God's anointed women are a blessing. God needs workers. Working in the ministry is hard work! It costs to follow Christ. Those who have been called by God to this work face many challenges.

Just as an attorney milks the cow when a husband and wife fight each other in a divorce, disagreement in the church only allows others to profit. We have lost a generation of young people, and there is no time for disagreement! And as Galatians 3:28 says, "In Christ Jesus … there is neither male nor female: for all are one in Christ Jesus."

Justice

Some say that God is not just,
But that's not true.
He doesn't love me any more
Than he loves you.
God expresses his love to each of us
By giving us time.
Your twenty-four hours each day
Is the same as mine.
Some squander their time with frivolous living,
Then blame God for the heartache
That that lifestyle has given.
Some abuse their bodies, their health, and time,
Then wonder why they don't have peace of mind!
But God has promised us in his Word,
For those of you who haven't heard,
That if you believe in Jesus and live true,
Heaven's gate will be open to you,
And if for Christ you labor and toil,
You will receive a just reward!
(For the Son of man shall come in the glory of his Father with His angels; and then he shall reward every man according To his works
(Matthew 16:27)

3

God's Prosperity

From a child, I was always taught that if one tithed (gave 10 percent of one's earnings to the church), one would be abundantly blessed. Give, give, give! Malachi 3:10 reads, "Bring ye all the tithes into the storehouse that there may be meat in my house … I will open you the windows of heaven and pour you out a blessing that there shall not be room enough to receive it." Second Corinthians 9:6 says, "He which soweth sparingly shall also reap sparingly, and he which soweth bountifully shall reap also bountifully." That is God's promise to believers, and God keeps his word. But what are the blessings? Are they always financial blessings? A job is a blessing, and food and shelter are the greatest blessing that God can bestow. Thousands are homeless today. To be provided with daily needs is a blessing.

God fed the Israelites manna from heaven while they journeyed through the wilderness. Some might call this the same old food every day. Yes, the food was the same the entire journey, but the Israelites were sustained—God provided for them in the wilderness. That was a blessing. They were also kept healthy: "Thy raiment waxed not old upon thee, neither did thy foot swell, these forty years" (Deuteronomy 8:4). God's promise to them was a homeland—shelter—and if obedient, they would get to eat until they were full: "When thou hast eaten and art full, then thou shalt bless the Lord thy God for the good land which he hath given thee" (Deuteronomy 8:10).

For Christians, earth is our pilgrimage. This is not our home; heaven is our promised land: "I go to prepare a place for you" (John 14:3). And God has promised us blessings if we are obedient. We will be provided for, given food and shelter. God knows how to bless and when to bless. He knows the heart: "The heart is deceitful ... and desperately wicked: who can know it?" (Jeremiah 17:9). Not everyone can handle material wealth or prosperity. Money can destroy if not used properly: "But they that will be rich fall into temptation and a snare, and into many foolish and hurtful lusts" (1 Timothy 6:9). The prodigal son had a lot of friends when he had money, but when he spent it all, his friends left also.

I have always paid my tithes, but I have never been blessed with a lot of money. However, the financial struggles in my life are the reason that I am relatively healthy today. I could not afford to eat out or to eat the rich foods that I enjoy. Rich foods and a lack of exercise can destroy one's earthly temple, the body. Eating fish, rice, beans, corn bread, and peanut-butter-and-jelly sandwiches and having to get around by walking kept me healthy. Some said that God was chastising me, but I was really being blessed. Health is a great blessing. Health means more than money. God may be preserving one's life by not supplying money for the foods and the automobile that one may be praying for. God knows best. If given an abundance of money today, which is not my heart's desire, I would know how to use it. (I sure hope that God is reading this page!) Today, there are foods that I enjoy but would not buy or eat even if I could afford to buy them. I know that they would rob me of health and make me gain excess weight that would also cause health problems. Medication is expensive.

One may pray for an automobile, but an automobile can also rob one of health. If a prayer for an automobile is not answered, remember that God knows best. Walking and riding a bike is exercise and will keep one healthy. Not receiving can also be a blessing from God, because health cannot be brought or restored when lost. Not being blessed with a lot of money preserved my health.

Many Christians would say that I was not blessed, but looking back over my life, I am thankful today that God did not give me some of the things I prayed for. During my younger years, I also prayed for a godly husband. I kept waiting and praying and waiting and praying, all while paying my tithes. I thought that my Prince Charming was on the way, and that hope gave me the strength to keep going. But many of you know or will find out later in life that God is long-suffering and takes his time. I was still paying my tithes and waiting for my blessing, though. Later in life, I decided that a husband was not what I really wanted, because I enjoy my freedom. Luckily, I was able to change that prayer in time! A husband was not what I really wanted, and God knew that from the beginning. Looking back over my life, I realize how blessed I was to get the opportunity to change that prayer before God got around to answering it. To have health and freedom in this stage of my life is a blessing!

When you think that God has not blessed you based on material things, remember that God has a reason for not giving us some things. I want to be in God's perfect will—not his permissive will. The world is having problems today because of people being in God's permissive will instead of his perfect will. The story of Abraham, Sarah, Isaac, and Ishmael in Genesis chapters 15 through 17 is representative of the differences between God's permissive will and perfect will. God's perfect will was for Abraham and Sarah to have a child together. However, because Abraham and Sarah believed Sarah was too old to have a child, Abraham instead had a child with Hagar, Sarah's handmaiden. This child, Ishmael, was a result of God's permissive will. Years later, Sarah and Abraham did have a child together, as God had intended. This child, Isaac, was God's perfect will. When you seek to be in God's perfect will, you are saying, "Not my will, but thine, be done" (Luke 22:42).

Unanswered Prayer

Thank you, God, for letting me live long enough to see
That I am much happier living close to thee.
I asked you for a husband many years ago,
But because you took your time and worked so slow,
The things I used to ask you for, I don't want anymore.
I have changed that prayer, dear Lord, and it is now my request

That you bless me with a good sound mind
And a reasonable portion of strength and health.
If you send that man to me now, Lord, I would not be his wife,
Because I no longer desire the things I once craved for
In this stage of my life.
So keep that man I asked you for, God.
Please don't send him to me,
For I am as happy as can be
When I wake up in the morning
And your loving face I see!

When we are committed and abide in God's Word, we will be blessed—God's way. "But seek ye first the kingdom of God, and his righteousness; and all these things shall be added unto you" (Matthew 6:33). Our needs will be met because that is his promise, and God cannot lie! "God is not a man that he should lie" (Numbers 23:19).

Also, many fail to realize that when God keeps one's mind strong through the storms of life, that, in and of itself, is a great blessing. Many break down mentally when the storms of life come, and trouble comes to all eventually. Some cannot take the pressures of life and commit suicide. Others have trouble sleeping at night and would pay any sum of money just to be able to get a good night's rest. Many in the body of Christ believe that most or all the blessings promised are material, but the spiritual and unseen blessings are the greatest blessings. A strong mind, the strength to face challenges, and a good night's sleep are just a few of God's blessings that are overlooked and seldom mentioned.

Material things can also be burdens. The maintenance and upkeep of property is time-consuming and can be burdensome. Years ago, I gave my car to my granddaughter. I got tired of taking it in for oil changes and driving it around the block to keep the battery strong when it was sitting for long periods of time. Public transportation for me is less expensive, and I can read, nap, and meet and witness to people on the bus—all with no stress. And walking to and from the bus stop is good exercise.

Earthly wealth has to be left behind, and there is the burden of making a will. Do you want to leave a lot of wealth behind? That wealth might be wasted, and money can destroy people. Look around at the reckless lifestyles of many of our youth. Do you really, in your heart, want to leave them more wealth that could destroy them? Pray over it. Leave them with eternal life instead. I want to see my children and grandchildren in heaven with me. They can eat beans as long as they know Jesus. One has to decide who to leave one's wealth to, and eventually that person has to will it to someone, and the cycle goes on and on. King Solomon summed it up in Ecclesiastes 1:14: "All is vanity and vexation of spirit."

There is an old saying that the best things in life are free. Money cannot buy any of these important things:

- salvation—"And none of them can by any means redeem his brother, nor give God a ransom for him" (Psalm 49:7).
- time—"And as it is appointed unto man once to die" (Hebrews 9:27).
- peace—"Great peace have they which love thou law: and nothing shall offend them" (Psalm 119:165). "And the peace of God, which passeth all understanding, shall keep your hearts and minds through Christ Jesus" (Philippians 4:7).
- health—"And every man that striveth for the mastery is temperate in all things" (1 Corinthians 9:25).
- sound mind—"For God hath not given us the spirit of fear; but of power and of love, and a sound mind" (2 Timothy 1:7).
- joy—"But the fruit of the spirit is love, joy, peace" (Galatians 5:22).

God wants us to have spiritual wealth—a testimony, something that edifies, that builds people. Many are hungry and thirsty for spiritual food—words that give hope, console, and strengthen. The spiritual hymns left behind are testimonies. Those testimonies came out of great emotional and physical suffering—hard trials! Horatio Spafford wrote the hymn "It Is Well with My Soul," after traumatic events in his life. The first was the death of his two-year-old son, and then the Great Chicago Fire of 1871 ruined him financially, as he was heavily invested in property that was destroyed. Then, when his wife and four daughters were crossing the Atlantic to Europe, their ship collided with another sea vessel, the *Loch Earn*, and sank rapidly. All four daughters died. His wife sent him a telegram that said, "Saved alone …" He and his wife later had three more children but also lost a four-year-old son to scarlet fever. Spafford's testimony, "It Is Well with My Soul," came out of great sorrow. His suffering was for divine purpose. His testimony has consoled millions for approximately 140 years. It was left behind for the collective body of Christ and can be found on the Internet and in practically all of the Baptist hymn books. The following is the first verse of the song:

> When peace like a river, attendeth my way,
> When sorrows like sea billows roll;
> Whatever my lot, Thou has taught me to say
> It is well, it is well, with my soul.

The Spaffords' Presbyterian church regarded their tragedy as divine punishment. Prosperity gospel can blind one from seeing Christ. There is also suffering for wrongdoing. For example, King David's suffering was chastisement for wrongdoing. But as Christians we cannot judge, because God is the only one who knows the why. He has told us in his Word to judge nothing before the time of his return. In other words, let it all go! Don't judge!

People

When I look at the folks that
I come in contact with every day,
I don't let the negative things
That they do and say
Affect me in any way.
I say to myself, *They're just dust, mortal, and clay.*
God is my judge, and I will stand before him one day
And answer for all that I think, do, and say!

> All go unto one place; all are dust, and all turn to dust again.
>
> —Ecclesiastes 3:21

> In God have I put my trust: I will not be afraid what man can do unto me.
>
> —Psalm 56:11

The mind-set for many in the body of Christ is that God's prosperity manifests in material wealth—if and when one tithes and gives financially. God can and may bless financially, but there are blessings far beyond money. Suffering ordained by God for spiritual wealth is the greatest blessing. The power to draw and inspire others comes through this spiritual wealth gained through suffering. Someone who has suffered or come through hard trials has a strong, powerful testimony. Salvation is a costly free gift because persecution and Christianity go hand in hand: "Yea, and all that live godly in Christ Jesus shall suffer persecution" (2 Timothy 3:12). The price for God's anointing power is suffering. The power company will give you as much electricity as you desire as long as the bill is paid. If you want an electrifying testimony, you must go through trials. Your trials and suffering make you able to effectively witness to and help others.

Remember that God will not put any more on you than you can bear. Some can bear more than others. Consider this little story about three crosses. One was plain, the second was covered with beautiful flowers, and the third was gorgeous, covered with the most beautiful roses. A person observing the crosses wanted the beautiful cross covered with roses but could not lift it, because of the thorns and thistles. The person moved on to the second cross, but it was too heavy to lift. Finally, the person tried the plain cross and was able to lift it. God gives us the crosses that we, individually, can bear. Be satisfied!

My dad often told this story: A bear and a man got into a fight. The man's wife was cheering for both the bear and her husband. When someone asked her why she was cheering for both sides, she said, "If my husband wins, I am going to have some meat, and if the bear wins, I am going to have some peace." You can't lose if you let God choose!

Now that I am seasoned, I can truthfully say that I believe God plays little jokes on us. He is trying to get us, individually, to the finish line. God knows that we don't need half of the things that we pray for, and sometimes he waits for us to change our own minds, as my poem "Unanswered Prayer" describes. Hope for a better day keeps one going. Trials and tribulations can lead to depression, substance abuse, reliance on medication, and so on. Some give up because they cannot see the end of the tunnel. Remember that God is not trying to destroy or break you down; the Holy Spirit wants to magnify himself through you! You will come out of the furnace of affliction without the smell of smoke if you keep the faith and don't give up. "When thou passest through the waters, I will be with thee; and through the rivers, they shall not overflow thee: when thou walkest through the fire, thou shalt not be burned; neither shall the flame kindle upon thee" (Isaiah 43:2). Remember the three Hebrew boys that Pharaoh threw into the furnace. He looked in the furnace and said, "Hey, I see four walking in the fire, and the fourth one looks like the Son of God." Others can be saved or drawn to Christ just by watching you go through trials with God's joy. Remember, the Holy Spirit will not take your joy—there is joy in suffering for Christ!

If the enemy comes and tries to take your job, *don't break down*—that is defeat. Have faith! All things work together for good. God has a purpose for allowing things to happen. "Greater is he that is in you, than he that is in the world" (1 John 4:4). Give your problems to Jesus. He will fight your battles: "And Moses said unto the people, Fear ye not, stand still, and see the salvation of the Lord ... The Lord shall fight for you, and ye shall hold your peace" (Exodus 14:13–14). God can divide the Red Sea and let you cross over on dry land. *Keep the faith!*

My dad used to say that none of the ingredients in a biscuit—flour, baking powder, baking soda, and shortening—can be eaten alone, but when everything is put together, you will have bread. Keep the faith!

The hymn "Amazing Grace," written by John Newton and first published in 1779, is another powerful testimony: "Thro' many dangers, toils, and snares I have already come; 'tis grace hath brought me safe thus far, and grace will lead me home." Romans 8:28 says, "And we know that all things work together for good to them that love the Lord." Never give up!

Life is similar to clothing. We sometimes outgrow clothes and have to buy a larger size. Because God is long-suffering, he can wait for us to grow and mature and outgrow our tears. I know from experience that if you stay with God, you will overcome and outgrow your tears. Sometimes I look back over my life and wonder and laugh at how I could have let such small things affect me like that. As Psalm 23:1–4 says, "The Lord is my shepherd, I shall not want. He maketh me to lie down in green pastures: he leadeth me beside the still waters. He restoreth my soul: he leadeth me in the paths of righteousness for his name's sake. Yea, though I walk through the valley of the shadow of death, I will fear no evil: for thou art with me."

As one matures, wants and desires change. God gave me enough hope to get me to where I am today, and today, I am all right. As Horatio Spafford's hymn says, "It is well, it is well, with my soul." If God had told me outright, from the beginning, that he was not going to answer my prayer, I probably would have broken down emotionally. I couldn't have handled it at that time. God kept me dangling. Whenever I reached a low ebb, he gave me enough hope in the form of songs, little messages, and small things to hold on to until I became strong in faith. It is like learning to walk—first comes crawling, then standing up, then baby steps, then walking, running, and skipping.

Realistically thinking, you can only wear one pair of shoes at a time, drive one automobile at a time, and hold so much food in your stomach at a time. Whether you eat beans or steak, both are filling, and both are protein. Too much food and unhealthful foods can send you to an early grave. Similarly, owning a lot of property can be a burden. You have to collect rent, take care of repairs, do taxes, and try to find good tenants, and in the end you will die and leave everything—all is vanity. Wealth can be a burden. Also, if you are given longevity of life, your health may not allow you to drive your car, maintain your property, or eat the foods you desire even if you have the money to do so.

We waste too much precious time and energy taking care of material things. Remember, we are given only twenty-four hours a day, and only what you do for Christ will last. Think about it. Your time on earth is the money that God has given you. How do you want to spend this wealth, your time? Time is precious. Once lost, it cannot be regained. Treasures in heaven must be earned—worked for. Do you want to invest your time in things that are temporal or things that are eternal? It has been said that if you lose money, you have lost nothing; if you lose your health, you have lost something; and if you lose time, you have lost all. Think about it!

Preparations

When my heart is heavy, and I am in despair,
I don't complain, because I know I am in the Lord's care.
The crosses and burdens that he gives me to bear
Are his way of helping me prepare
To lose sight of this world and enjoy spiritual rest,
Because true happiness is not found in the things we possess
But in making preparations to meet him one day
And being kind to others and giving him glory
And praise in all we think, do, and say!

Poor yet Rich

One can be poor yet rich. Peter and John, two of Jesus's disciples, did not have wealth. They were broke. Yet they possessed true riches, riches that gave life—the name of Jesus. Revelation 3:18 says, "I counsel thee to buy of me gold tried in the fire, that thou mayest be rich."

The man at the temple gate begging for alms wanted money, but money was not what he needed. "And a certain man lame from his mother's womb was carried, who they laid daily at the gate of the temple ... to ask alms ... Then Peter said, Silver and gold have I none; but such as I have give I thee: In the name of Jesus Christ of Nazareth rise up and walk" (Acts 3:2, 3:6).

My Story

I am rich! I don't say this to a lot of people, because you know how some people are—if they think you have a lot of money, they always want to borrow from you and never pay you back. Do not let the thrift store clothes that I wear fool you—I am very wealthy.

I was on a tour bus at Martha's Vineyard some years ago, and most of the people on the bus were well dressed. As you may have guessed, I had on tennis shoes and thrift store clothing. Sometimes people look down on you when you're dressed in this attire. As we were riding along, I said loudly, "My Father owns all of this."

One man abruptly turned around and said, "He does?"

I said, "Yes, he does," but I was not talking about my earthly father. I was referring to my heavenly Father.

I am an heir—a joint heir with Christ. I am rich! However, God has me on a budget. I wouldn't mind if he increased my allowance, because the cost of living is high, but I am satisfied. He puts my wealth in my heavenly bank account because he doesn't want it stolen. My wealth is waiting for me. In the meantime, I am trying to earn more because God pays great dividends. James 2:2–4 reads, "For if there come unto your assembly a man with a gold ring, in goodly apparel, and there come in also a poor man in vile raiment; And ye have respect to him that weareth the gay clothing, and say unto him, Sit thou here in a good place; and say to the poor, Stand thou there … Are ye not then partial in yourselves, and are become judges of evil thoughts?"

For the homeless and those who have fallen by the wayside, look up! Have faith! Never feel that you are alone. God will, if you trust him, take care of you. The blessings he provides may not be what you want or desire, but they will be what you need. Jesus also walked in your shoes. Jesus was not welcome in the inn and was born in a stable. He also was homeless: "And Jesus saith unto him, the foxes have holes, and the birds of the air have nests; but the Son of man hath not where to lay his head" (Matthew 8:20). Jesus was poor: "For ye know the grace of our Lord Jesus Christ, that though he was rich, yet for your sakes he became poor, that ye through his poverty might be rich" (2 Corinthians 8:9). And to make matters worse, God, his Father, made him work, and not only did he have to work, but he also was not given a professional, white-collar position. Jesus was a carpenter, a blue-collar worker: "Is not this the carpenter, the son of Mary?" (Mark 6:3). And to add insult to injury, after a life of toil and grief, he had to go to Calvary to die for you and me. That's love!

> Greater love hath no man, than this that a man lay down his life for his friends.
>
> —John 15:13

> For God so loved the world, that he gave his only begotten Son, that whosoever believeth in him should not perish, but have everlasting life.
>
> —John 3:16

Dear God
You have made me struggle
All the way,
Every time I get a Cent!
Something comes along
And takes it away.
I am not complaining
God Because I know that
Some Sweet Day,
I will meet you in Heaven
And there you will say –
I kept you broke
So that you would stay,
Close beside me
All the way!

4

The Church

The true church has no walls—it is not made of brick and mortar. It is a spiritual house made of people—the body of Christ. It was foretold that the Branch (Jesus) would build the church: "Thus speaketh the Lord of hosts, saying, behold the man whose name is the Branch, and he shall grow up out of his place, and he shall build the temple of the Lord" (Zechariah 6:12).

Jesus is the chief cornerstone and the head of the church. However, inside the head is the brain—the seat of all knowledge. God is the brain of the body. We people in the body of Christ, individually and collectively, are God's temple. We have different functions, but we are all connected. None of the parts of the natural body work alone. The natural body works in harmony. This is even more the case with the spiritual body. The body never argues with the head (God). When the head makes a decision to do something, the body responds accordingly. The body moves with the head. There are no meetings or discussions, and the head does not consult with the body. The head's decisions are final. God does not seek approval from the body.

We people in the body of Christ have different functions, but our agenda is the same—to save a dying world. We are all connected. Christ is not divided. All parts of the natural body are needed and necessary for perfect functioning. The same is true of the spiritual body of Christ. There is no schism in the body of Christ., "For by one Spirit are we all baptized into one body ... That there should be no schism in the body; but that the members should have the same care one for another" (1 Corinthians 12:13, 12:25).

If the heart decided to stop functioning, the body would die. Similarly, if the colon, which helps to rid the body of waste, decided to stop functioning, the body would perish as surely as it would if the heart stopped working. All members are important, and one is not honored above the other. The natural body does not fight against itself. The hands never beat up the head or feet because they disagree. They work together. Without feet, the body cannot move. The same applies to the spiritual house. There are parts of my natural body that I have never seen, but I know that they are there because I can't function without them.

The Holy Spirit is not in the building; it is in the people—the members of the body of Christ. As members of the body of Christ, we individually and collectively may not understand or agree with some of the gifts and anointings, but if we all are working for the same cause—the same agenda—all gifts and anointings are connected to the body. We can be on different roads as long as the destination is the same. We cannot fight against or disagree with members of the same body, whether male or female, because we are all connected—soldiers killing soldiers. One does not argue or fight against God, the head. When God chooses and anoints, can we as the body of Christ reject his callings? I don't reject, dislike, or hate any of my body parts, even those that I have never seen, because I need them if I want to function, to be able to walk and talk.

When one professes to be in the body of Christ but comes with a message other than the death, burial, and resurrection of Jesus and my spirit does not bear witness, then I know in my spirit that that person is not a member of the body. First Corinthians 12:13 says, "For by one Spirit are we all baptized into one body."

God speaks of oneness—Father, Son, Holy Spirit, these three are one. Jesus said, "I and my Father are one" (John 10:30). God the Father, God the Son, and God the Holy Spirit are one—the brain, the eyes, and the head. The brain is God the Father, the seat of all knowledge; the Holy Spirit is the eyes; and Jesus, the Son of God, is the head of the church. This was the honor bestowed upon Jesus for giving his life. "And hath put all things under his feet, and gave him to be the head over all things the church, Which is his body" (Ephesians 1:22–23). Jesus received the highest honor, and he is the password to heaven: "For the Father judgeth no man, but hath committed all judgment unto the Son: That all men should honour the Son" (John 5:22–23)

The Holy Spirit—the eyes of the church—does the work. The natural eyes carry light and images to the brain; the eyes have their function, but by themselves they do not see. It is the brain that sees. God is the seat of it all—the brain of it all. Remember, God (the Father) sent Jesus (the Son) and knew all things because the Holy Spirit was with him in full. Abraham, Isaac, and Jacob follow the same pattern. Abraham was the father of faith, Isaac was the heir, and Jacob, who was changed, is symbolic of the Holy Spirit. God's oneness is not the same as ours. God has one body of born-again believers, yet John saw a number that no man could number: "After this I beheld and, lo, a great multitude, which no man could number, of all nations, and kindreds, and people, and tongues, stood before the throne" (Revelation 7:9). That is God's oneness, one body of born-again believers. The natural body has one brain that controls all, and God, through his Son, Jesus, controls all. There is one head (Jesus), which can be seen; one brain (God), which cannot be seen inside the head; and one body—all perfectly connected. Without a brain, the body is useless. All are connected! God has one salvation plan, one agenda—Jesus: "For there is none other name under heaven given among men, whereby we must be saved" (Acts 4:12).

The music ministry is powerful. I am a lover of the arts. If God had given me the privilege of choosing a gift, I would have chosen music or art. Music is a universal language. Music is therapy, especially in the midnight hour. I read in a book that our true leaders are not the politicians and elected officials but the musicians, writers, and artists and those in ministry. I totally agree with this idea. Think about it—these latter individuals are the ones God uses to help, inspire, and change people. Realistically speaking, under normal circumstances, how many people wake up in the morning with politicians on their minds? However, we do pray for the leaders of the world because they make decisions that affect daily life. The influence has been given to the body of Christ—the church—and collectively, we have let politicians get on God's turf. And now they are changing laws that affect Christianity. In some government workplaces Christmas carols can no longer be sung and Jesus's name no longer mentioned. What have we collectively done? Has the body of Christ lost its influence? Have we sold out? Politicians are elected by the people and for the people to represent the will of the people. At election time, many politicians quote a few scriptures and put on a show of being Christian to win the people, but is that of God? The body needs the spirit of discernment. "No man that warreth entangles himself with the affairs of this life; that he may please him who hath chosen himself to be a soldier" (2 Timothy 2:4. "Greater is he that is in you, than he that is in the world" (1 John 4:4).

God revealed to me a few years ago that he wanted me to attend a particular church. Being human, I did not want to go, so I cried about it. However, in the midnight hour God woke me up with the words to the song "Just Think of His Goodness to You." The Holy Spirit speaks to my spirit sometimes with a song. I immediately went downstairs to look up the song in my hymn book to see what God was saying. These are some of the words to that hymn by R. C. Ward:

> When waves of affliction sweep over the soul,
> And sunlight is hidden from view,
> If ever you're tempted to fret or complain,
> Just think of his goodness to you.

God did not ask me to do anything big—it was a simple assignment. God has been good to me, and God reminded me of that. I am not worthy of the many blessings that he has bestowed upon me.

In the apostle Paul's day, Christians (the church) met in different homes ("Salute the brethren … which is in his house" [Colossians 4:15]). They did not have the New Testament Bible as we have it today. Paul taught by letters—the epistles: "I wrote unto you in an epistle" (1 Corinthians 5:9).

The church can be just two or three members: "For where two or three are gathered together in my name, there am I in the midst of them" (Matthew 18:20). God does not need a crowd to accomplish his purpose. Remember the story of Gideon in Judges 7:6–8. "The people that are with thee are too many for me to give the Midianites into their hands, lest Israel vaunt themselves against me, saying Mine own hand hath saved me" (Judges 7:2).

The true church is about ministry. Our works are going to be tried by fire. If any person's works burn, he or she will receive no reward. Earthly buildings will be destroyed, and rewards will be given for what was and is done for Christ. We do not know who will be rewarded or for what. One may bring in a harvest that is the result of someone else's labor: "I sent you to reap that whereon ye bestowed no labour; other men labored, and ye are entered into their labours" (John 4:38). In this life, people sometimes reap rewards and take credit for things that belong to others—songs, plays, books, inventions, and so on. They may reap the earthly reward, but the heavenly reward cannot be taken and, unlike the temporal earthly reward, the heavenly reward is eternal. Since we are human, it is easy to become upset about these things, but it is important to let it all go because no one can steal the eternal reward.

God, in his awesome wisdom, does not let people keep the records. Human nature makes people partial, but God is no respecter of persons: "Of a truth, I perceive that God is no respecter of persons" (Acts 10:34). "But he that doeth wrong shall receive for the wrong which he hath done: and there is no respect of persons" (Colossians 3:25). No one will have to shed tears regarding unfair treatment, because God is a just God. Jesus is the righteous judge. Everything is and has been recorded. God has a Department of Justice. No one is going to escape. One may shed tears down here on earth, but this life will come to an end, and we, as Christians—the body of Christ—will live in a world that is fair and just: "Weeping may endure for a night, but joy cometh in the morning" (Psalm 30:5); "That which is crooked cannot be made straight" (Ecclesiastes 1:15); and "He hath appointed a day, in the which he will judge the world in righteousness by that man whom he hath ordained" (Acts 17:31).

One's name *must* be written in the Book of Life if one wants to enter heaven. Skin color, money, prestige, accolades, degrees, and so on, will not get one into heaven. There is only one entrance—the door called Jesus Christ. One must be saved—born again! And being saved is an individual choice. No one man or woman has been given the power to save. We as a body can only individually and collectively lift up Jesus and extend the invitation to discipleship. The power to save is not ours. No man or woman can save his or her children, mother, father, sister, brother, or friends. God knows that humankind would be partial if given the power to make such decisions.

Works

Many of us went to church when we were young, but many of our churches did not have works. Money was given to foreign missions, but members were not involved in individual and collective ministries. Christians also have a work to do at home—that is where our work starts. There are many churches that are doing great works at home and abroad.

Our nation is crumbling. When I see things in my home crumbling and in need of repair, I fix them or call someone who can. If I didn't, my house would eventually fall down. God has given all believers the authority to do ministry: "Whatsoever thy hand findeth to do, do it with thy might; for there is no work in the grave" (Ecclesiastes 9:10).

My dad preached a lifetime to mostly the same congregation, but the calling of the body of Christ goes beyond the Sunday-morning service. A body is suppose to have ministries—ministering at prisons and nursing homes, visiting the sick and shut-in, getting involved in the community, and so on. This is the mission of the church, or the body of Christ. Read. "For I was an hungred, and ye gave me no meat: I was thirsty, and ye gave me no drink: I was a stranger, and ye took me not in; naked, and ye clothed me not: sick, and in prison, and ye visited me not" (Matthew 25:42–43).

The Bible speaks of planting, watering, and sowing seeds. If there is going to be a harvest, there has to be labor. The body of Christ individually and collectively cannot reap a harvest unless we go into the vineyard of life (the world) and labor: "The harvest truly is plenteous, but the labourers are few; Pray ye therefore the Lord of the harvest, that he will send forth laborers into his harvest" (Matthew 9:37–38). If we are waiting for our youth to decide to come in on their own, we may be waiting a long time. James 2:17 says, "Even so faith, if it hath not works, is dead, being alone." There is no earthly recognition or offering plate in street ministry or similar ministries (shelters, nursing homes, and so on), but God is the paymaster. God will reward!

There is a story about a man who bought a run-down, dilapidated farm. With a lot of hard work, he fixed it up and planted a garden.

His friend came by one day and said, "Look what the Lord has done."

The man responded, "The Lord did not do all of that by himself; I helped."

We can plant and water, but God gives the increase. Our rewards will be waiting for us when we get to heaven: "Lay not up for yourselves treasures upon earth … But lay up for yourselves, treasures in heaven" (Matthew 6:19–20).

The Christian life is not a life of bliss; it is a life of toil, trials, afflictions, and persecutions, but we already have the victory—we are more than conquerors. Jesus won at Calvary: "But be of good cheer; I have overcome the world" (John 16:33). The world has been judged; we are just fighting some battles down here—good versus evil.

Here's another story: A preacher died and went to heaven. God was passing out rewards, but when he got to the preacher, God said, "No reward."

In his amazement the preacher said to God, "No reward? You didn't see me on the cover of *Time* magazine and on national TV."

God said, "I saw you—and that was your reward."

As Matthew 6:1 says, "Take heed that ye do not your alms before men, to be seen of them: otherwise ye have no reward of your Father which is in heaven."

You may face rejection when working in the harvest and not only in the harvest; rejection can also come from loved ones who are not committed or not interested in godly things. However, God's Word does not return void. It accomplishes what God sent it to do. All the seeds planted will not come up in our lifetime. God knows those who are going to accept him in the final hour. Many ball games have been won in the ninth inning. Christ can be accepted silently in the heart, and only God can see the heart. We, the body of Christ, do not know who is going to be saved in the end. Our job is to plant the seeds. No one but God knows how a seed will grow. God will send someone else to water, but he gives the increase. We are all connected. Just as in the planting of an earthly seed, someone has to dig up the soil and get it ready to receive the seed. Planting spiritual seeds is a united effort, and according to Psalm 126:5, "They that sow in tears shall reap in joy."

The Church Should Have a Vision

Proverbs 29:18 says, "Where there is no vision, the people perish." A vision energizes—keeps one going. Looking forward to a future endeavor keeps one striving and motivated. I am writing this book because my vision for the body of Christ is for us to lay aside our differences, individually and collectively, and work together in harmony to bring in a great harvest before the second coming of Christ. He is coming! The signs that Jesus told us to watch for are here. The fig tree has blossomed. The great commission is to go into all the world and preach the gospel of Jesus Christ. We have complicated salvation when it is simple. God's salvation plan is what saves. Doctrine does not save. The thief on the cross, crucified with Jesus, only believed that Jesus was the Son of God, and he instantly received eternal life—in the final hour!

We have lost a generation of young people. The problem with our youth as a whole is that they have not been taught. We cannot teach if we cannot draw them in. The first priority, however, is salvation. For this generation and the times that they are living in, my vision for the body of Christ is practical teaching—a practical religion. We need teachings that apply to everyday life. Our youth should know that in life, the real world, people are not going to pamper them. One needs tough skin to survive. Second Timothy 3:12 says, "Yea, and all that will live godly in Christ Jesus shall suffer persecution." The anger displayed in family disputes could possibly be calmed down if our young people were taught God's way of handling anger, a God-given emotion. Proverbs 15:1 teaches one how to handle anger: "A soft answer turneth away wrath: but grievous words stir up anger." And Ephesians 4:26 says, "Be ye angry, and sin not. Let not the sun go down upon your wrath." Many scriptures provide practical knowledge, and such wisdom could save one's life.

The Christian life is not easy. There has to be a change of lifestyle—a walk in the newness of life. A lifestyle change takes time; it is a process. Years ago, we did not have the counseling that we have today, but we were better off back then. People talked to each other. In fact, in a conversation I had with a Spanish instructor many years ago, she expressed that in her country they don't have the mental health problems that we have in our nation, because people talk to each other. In our society, many feel that people are not trustworthy and not sincere.

When I was young, we were corrected and taught the commonsense values that youth do not have today. And everyone helped! It takes a village. What has happened to us? Is it because we are not doing things God's way? Godly correction would fix many of the major problems that we are having with children. It is sad to say that today when a parent tries to correct his or her uncontrollable child, those around call the police or family services. Do these people really love the child? Children are taught by the worldly system that their parents cannot touch them. How did we as a collective body let the world get away with imposing these laws? Is it about money, or is it about love? Children will, if not corrected, end up in court, prison, therapists' offices, and so on. And the criminal justice system brutally corrects.

We have millions of professing born-again believers attending church Sunday after Sunday while the world, the school system, and our youth are being destroyed. Forgive me, but why not put all the church folk to work? We have turned our society over to our youth, but young people do not have the wisdom and understanding needed. Wisdom is with the ancient—the experienced: "With the ancient is wisdom, and in length of days understanding" (Job 12:12). Our nation, as a whole, does not respect the elderly as other nations do, but we should: "The hoary head [gray] is a crown of glory, if it be found in the way of righteousness" (Proverbs 16:31).

We have enough saints in the body to have an understanding mother in every elementary school classroom to help nurture the little ones. Teachers need help, and many of those in charge, even though well educated, lack the God-given wisdom and understanding that it takes to work with children. Our society wants the little ones to sit and be fed information, but children are not designed to sit attentively and act with the understanding of an adult. That is the reason God told us to "train up a child in the way he should go" (Proverbs 22:6). We as a collective body have been too silent on the subject. A dog has to be trained.

My little one once told me, "If you spank me, I'll call 911." She probably wouldn't have been able to pick up the phone and dial the number, but an ungodly system has taught our children that such a thing is an option. Thank God that my dad has gone to glory; otherwise, I would probably be visiting him in prison! When my dad said, "Sit down," he meant it, and he did not repeat himself. If my dad were alive today, he would be correcting the youth in his small congregation regarding the dress code. If any of my brothers had tried to leave home with their pants so low that their underwear showed, like many of our youth do today, or if I had gone out half-naked with my breasts showing, it would have been the end of time for us. My dad did not play! He said what he meant, and he meant what he said. He also said, "When you get locked up, don't call me, because I am teaching you right from wrong."

Many children today are out of control because they have not received godly correction and laws today punish parents who try to correct in God's way. Again, I am not speaking here about abuse, and I am speaking about normal children who will not listen. I am not referring to children who are mentally challenged, have disabilities, or have suffered abuse. Verbal correction and denying privileges is a better way of correcting if this fixes the behavior.

Many children have not been taught to honor parents. Parents make mistakes too. But God's commandment to honor one's parents came directly from God; it is one of the Ten Commandments given to Moses. This commandment also comes with a promise: "Honour thy father and thy mother: that thy days may be long upon the land which the Lord thy God giveth" (Exodus 20:12). It troubles my spirit when I see TV judges belittle a parent in front of his or her child even when a parent is justifiably brought to court. To me, such behavior sends the wrong message to our youth. I think people should pray before taking their parents to court and let God handle the situation if possible.

Laws have been put in place for the truly abused. Spanking an out-of-control child is not abuse. In my day teachers used paddles, and parents used switches from trees, and those switches left little marks. And correction was done on the scene. If a child acted out in the store or in school, that was where they were corrected. If a parent tried that today, he or she would be put in jail. Children have short-term memories. Many times after arriving home, they have forgotten what they did wrong.

Today, I know the difference between right and wrong, good and bad, and respect and disrespect because I was corrected. It is better to be corrected by the rod of a parent than the rod of God. I am sure that many of you have been told to use tough love. In the Old Testament, God used tough love for rebellious children, having them stoned to death: "If a man have a stubborn and rebellious son, which will not obey the voice of his father, or the voice of his mother, and that, when they have chastened him, will not hearken unto them ... And all of the men of his city shall stone him with stones, that he die: so shalt thou put evil away from among you; And all Israel shall fear and hear" (Deuteronomy 21:18, 21:21). If God had not given such tough love, children as a whole would have been out of control, as today's children are. Youth need to know that godly correction is not child abuse. A dog has to be trained, and so do children: "Foolishness is bound in the heart of a child; but the rod of correction shall drive it far from him" (Proverbs 22:15). "Withhold not correction from the child: for if thou beatest him with the rod, he shall not die" (Proverbs 23:13). God corrects: "For whom the Lord loveth he chasteneth" (Hebrews 12:6). I am speaking of godly correction, not of abuse or of beating a child unmercifully or because one is angry.

The criminal justice system brutally corrects bad behavior. A judge will have a disorderly person acting out in the courtroom restrained, handcuffed, and locked up, and police do not shoot to wound but to kill.

In prison some inmates are placed in solitary confinement, which has damaging psychological effects. Many years ago, I watched a TV show on which a minister said that his son had been killed in prison because he had been involved in a fight and, to break up fights, the guards shoot to kill. Now that's brutality.

My vision is that we, as the body of Christ, win our youth back and teach them that an ungodly system does not love. If the world is sincere and its concern for our children is out of love, then why do law enforcement officers carry weapons, and why do prison guards shoot and kill offenders? Why don't police officers and prison guards talk with offenders and tell them to make better choices? That is what the system wants godly parents to do. Equal treatment! Lawbreakers are someone's loved ones. So sit offenders down when they pull out a weapon and talk with them—tell them that their behavior is unacceptable and talk to them about bad choices. Give them a time-out. Don't beat and shoot them; instead, take their privileges away—no TV, no Internet, no phone calls. After all, that is what the law requires parents to do with uncontrollable children. An old saying goes, "What is good for the goose won't kill the gander." Children are going to be uncontrollable until they are taught and then corrected—God's way. As the twig is bent, so grows the tree. We as the body of Christ can and should be involved. When law enforcement officers lay down their weapons, we will put our rods of correction away. That is what one calls equal rights!

How did we, as the body of Christ, let the world get away with imposing laws that interfere with Christian family values? Those with a different philosophy, who do not believe in the rod of correction, are imposing their beliefs on *all*. Many of today's children just need an old-fashioned spanking. I respect the rights of those who believe differently, and those individuals should respect the rights of others as well. The psychiatrist Fritz Perls said, "I do my thing and you do your thing. I am not in this world to live up to your expectations, and you are not in this world to live up to mine. You are you, and I am I, and if by chance we find each other, it's beautiful. If not, it can't be helped." Medication is not the answer for normal children. They do not come into the world knowing how to behave. We have to train them. "Train up a child in the way he should go: and when he is old, he will not depart from it" (Proverbs 22:6). "When I was a child, I spake as a child, I understood as a child, I thought as a child: but when I became a man, I put away childish things" (1 Corinthians 13:11). It irritates me to see a system try to force its way of parenting on all. You cannot put everyone in the same basket. One must study a child's personality. Some children can be talked to, and others cannot. The rod has to be used.

God is creating children for different purposes in life. A child's will can also be broken, so the goal is to chastise but not totally break the will. A stubborn trait could be an asset that God uses later, but the child must be brought into subjection to follow rules, do what is correct, and respect authority. Otherwise, that child will suffer in life and possibly get shot for disobeying the law. A child can have an opinion as far as I am concerned. Someone asked me once if I would rather be a jackass or a horse. A horse will go into battle and lose his life, but a jackass won't because of its stubborn streak.

God has told us as godly parents how to discipline and raise our children if we believe and follow his teachings. God knows what is in human nature; he created us. God does not force Christianity upon us but gives us a choice. We can choose to accept or reject salvation, Jesus. God knows that he is the creator of all humankind and that it is his air that we are breathing. He knows that we will see him one day, face-to-face, and that many of us will have regrets. There is no argument. However, God still allows us to choose who we will serve. That's love!

Practical Knowledge

The book of Proverbs speaks of not meddling in strife that does not belong to you: "He that passeth by, and meddleth with strife belonging not to him, is like one that taketh a dog by the ears" (Proverbs 26:17). Just this year, I have seen news stories about people who have lost their lives trying to help in disputes not belonging to them, trying to help someone else. That's just how true God's Word is—it's practical wisdom.

I am going to share something personal with you: I have a spiritual gift. My dad told me that you cannot always share spiritual gifts with others, because some people will think that you are crazy. I want all of you to know that I am of sound mind. I have all my marbles upstairs, but God sometimes speaks to me in dreams. I use to love passing out comic book Bible tracts to teens, and in the past, when I would see teens fighting outside, I would try to break up the fights and talk to them. Then one night in a dream, I was trying to break up a fight between two teens, but one of the teens shot me and then turned back around and continued fighting. The dream bothered me, so I casually mentioned it to a young man, and he told me that he carried a gun. God freed me instantly from breaking up fights. I am not the police. I will call 911.

One of my favorite practical-wisdom scriptures is Proverbs 25:17: "Withdraw thy foot from thy neighbour's house; lest he be weary of thee, and so hate thee." In other words, if you visit your neighbor too often, he or she will get tired of seeing you.

Wholeness

My vision for the body of Christ is also that we teach wholeness. God is not only concerned with the spiritual man and woman; he is also concerned with the temple, the earthly house—the body. We individually exemplify Christ; we are his representatives in the world. Bad habits that destroy the temple of God—too much food, alcohol, drugs, lust, and so on—affect one's ministry. It is difficult to work when the physical body is not well. That is time lost. God, just as an earthly employer, needs individuals who are available and physically able to work. When an employer fires an individual for constantly calling in sick, it is not personal. Someone has to show up who can get the job done!

The earthly body is not designed to last forever. It's like an automobile. No matter how well maintained an automobile is, it is going to eventually die. However, a well-maintained automobile will last longer and run better. Constantly taking it in for repair is costly and time-consuming. The same is true for the human body. Health care is expensive, and going to the doctor's office and having lab work done takes up a lot of time. When health is lost due to neglect and abuse, it may never be regained. My vision is that the collective body of Christ teach wholeness and a disciplined lifestyle.

I enjoy food and eating, but I know when to back away. It is my responsibility to bring my body and mind into subjection with prayer and God's help. Part of my personal discipline is a limit of gaining no more than five extra pounds. Losing five pounds is difficult for me, so one hundred pounds would be almost impossible. It is not food in general that puts the weight on but bad choices in food, like high-fat foods, and a lack of exercise. One will not live a day longer than God intended, but a good quality of life is a blessing. Food addictions can cause poverty ("For the drunkard and the glutton shall come to poverty" [Proverbs 23:21]), loss of limbs (due to diabetes), blindness, heart problems, knee problems, back problems, and so on. Such self-induced illnesses should be avoided. Of course, some illnesses are brought on by Father Time and cannot be avoided.

The Bible also warns about overindulgence of alcohol. According to Proverbs 20:1, "Wine is a mocker, strong drink is raging; and whosoever is deceived thereby is not wise." They had liquor and wine in Old Testament times: "Thou shalt not delay to offer the first of thy ripe fruits, and of thy liquors" (Exodus 22:29). The Bible states that a little wine is good for you: "Drink no longer water, but use a little wine for thy stomach's sake" (1 Timothy 5:23). But moderation in all things! "But be not drunk with wine, wherein in excess" (Ephesians 5:18). Drinking becomes a problem when one is drinking to forget, to gain peace of mind. When one sobers up, the problems will be there waiting, and a new problem will have been added. Alcohol is expensive, alters behavior, affects health, and more. Take your burdens to God and leave them there. You and I can't fix the problems that come into our lives, and worry will destroy our health. My suggestion is to let Jesus worry about your problems. Give your problems to him!

Many years ago, I had this job that I desperately needed, but the young supervisor was getting to me and making me stressed. Then one day I was at the library, and God led me to a certain self-help book.

The first chapter started out, "You cannot change another person." The only person that one can change is oneself. If God has problems with rebellion, where does that leave me—us? People seldom change. When you are struggling with someone, God is not going to change the other person; he wants to change you. Your home, work, or family situation may never change, but *you* will be different. You will view life or see people from a different perspective—you will have a changed attitude and be more accepting. Accept the things you cannot change, and one thing that you cannot change is another person. God wants to change our perspectives on life. People have hurts, heartaches, problems, and needs, and what they reflect out—what we see with the natural eye—may not be the real person. Some people are not strong, and only God knows what they are facing in their personal lives. Health also affects attitude. God wants us to have understanding hearts. That is my prayer to God, like King Solomon's—give me an understanding heart! I have not arrived yet, but I am on my way.

Many years ago, I would sit in the lounge at work during my lunch break and chitchat with a young woman. She later stopped talking to me, and when I saw her in the hall, she would go the other way. I was deeply hurt and wondered what I had said or done to offend her. Well, a few years later, while shopping, I heard someone call my name and turned around to see this young woman. She said that she had been in the hospital for a year because of a nervous breakdown. She also said, "I'm all right now!" One never knows. "Forgive, and ye shall be forgiven" (Luke 6:37).

Everyone that truly knows me knows that I am plainspoken and spontaneous—those traits just come naturally. That is my personality, but I am working on it. My dad had a difficult personality, and one could say that I am a chip off the old block. My father was difficult to deal with, but I understood him and loved him in spite of his flaws. When my father had his heart attack, he refused to let his doctor examine him. The doctor had to wait for me to come because I knew how to handle my father. For example, I knew that my father was afraid of needles, so if he was refusing to eat, I would tell the doctor or nurse, so that my father could hear, that they should feed him intravenously or give him a shot.

As much as my father and I fought (verbally, not physically), he would always do what I said. Deep down, he greatly respected me. He just could not accept strong-minded women. He lived in a man's world. He always started our fights. I would visit him at his home smoking my peace pipe, but he couldn't accept that. He always wanted my opinion about something, and once I gave it, it would start a fight. I speak my mind! I am not a hypocrite. I don't wear two hats. I am what I am. No one would argue with my father or dispute what he said because he was a man of God. I was the only one who would challenge him. It helped him grow. My dad was a warhorse, and so am I. He didn't back down, and neither do I. But he needed a challenge. My mother always let him have his way—right or wrong. So he needed to be around someone like me to keep his blood pumping. There is an old saying "I may not be right, but I'm never wrong." When everyone agrees with everything that one says and does, one cannot grow. For growth, one must be exposed to different perspectives. My mother, who has passed on, said that my dad and I gave her high blood pressure, but I think it was the fried chicken that she ate practically every day. I don't know what is going to happen when I get to heaven. Hopefully God will put my dad and me in separate rooms. There is an old spiritual "Plenty Good Room," and I hope that is the truth.

There is a treasure of wealth in books. I read a lot. To me, reading is the same as talking to another person. People are books. Remember, all members in the body have different functions. Learn from the hand, the heart, and so on. You may be the head, but the other members have contributions to make also. The head alone is useless. Where is your head going to go without a body to carry it around? It needs the other parts of the body to function. We learn from all. My old boss used to tell me that the dumbest person in the world can teach you something.

The Bible does not specifically mention many of the drugs that are so destructive today, but from observation, it's clear that drugs destroy the mind and the body. Some herbs have divine purpose and are used in medication, but anything that alters behavior and can cause death and problems with the law is not of God. This teaching should start with our youth as a wholeness gospel. We need to teach youth the consequences of bad choices.

Schools have taken the responsibility of teaching children, with parental approval, about their bodies, sex, and relationships as early as elementary school. However, are they teaching God's way? I do not want to go against the grain, but I am old school. While I feel that there is an appropriate time for children to learn about nature and sex, I personally find teaching dating in fifth and sixth grade troubling. There are different points of view on this subject, however. As the body of Christ, are we teaching children about God's principles regarding sex, alcohol abuse, drugs, and so on, or are we leaving that responsibility to the worldly system? Have we lost it as a nation? My mother would say we're going out of the world backward. Individually and collectively as the body of Christ we have failed to teach and, most importantly, set a good example for our children when it comes to sex, drugs, alcohol abuse, and so on. Flesh has to be brought into subjection! The flesh cannot be fed everything that it desires. Discipline is necessary.

Sex comes with responsibilities and consequences that young people are not ready for. For example, how can two teenagers financially support and raise a child they brought into the world while still children themselves? How about paying doctor bills for sexually contracted diseases? Teenagers are not ready for such responsibility, so instead the burden falls on parents and taxpayers. If and when one brings a child into the world, one must be equipped to support that child.

I tell my great-grandson that his first paycheck will go to child support. If a man gets too far behind in child support payments, he cannot get a passport, his driver's license is affected, and he can be locked up. And the woman is free! Equal treatment—God is just! The man is punished through child support more than the woman when a child is born out of wedlock. Why punish the man with large child support payments? The man, unless he makes a large sum of money, suffers from these payments. It takes two to tango. The woman did not have to say yes. Also, the woman has the enjoyment of her child or children, her paycheck, and support money. I enjoyed raising my children, and I enjoy being with my grandchildren. Men were created differently. King Solomon had seven hundred wives and three hundred concubines (1

Kings 11:3). We know that the brain should be in the head, but that takes time. Men should read Proverbs 7 in its entirety. Teach the youth—that is my vision. "And beheld among the simple ones, I discerned among the youth, a young man void of understanding" (Proverbs 7:7).

When people have children young, they miss out on a stage of life that they should be enjoying—going to college, attending football games, and so on. Many who missed out on their childhoods try to recuperate later in life. I am sure that many of you have seen elders trying to dress and act like young people and going to clubs and so on. The Bible says the old folks, the elderly, should teach the young, but some of them are instead trying to get their teen years back. But when one misses the natural stages of life, it is like an old tree that comes up crooked. An old, crooked tree cannot be straightened; it has to be cut down. We as the body should, when appropriate, let the young people know that God is not pleased with the direction that they are going. When someone can support his or her habits, then that is between that person and God. But if the burden falls on the shoulders of parents, grandparents, and taxpayers, then others have the right to dictate and speak. If things are made tougher for youth who are living reckless lives, some may think twice before they make bad decisions.

Some may say, "I will just have an abortion." Wholeness gospel teaches that we have to live with all the decisions we make in life. God is a forgiving God, but I have met people who have had difficulty living with themselves because of choices that they made while young. I met a young woman fifty-plus years ago who told me that she got high off drugs to try to forget her past. She told me that the abortions she'd had in life haunted her and that she could not sleep at night. I also once met a young woman who had left her children to be raised by her mother. I asked her if that bothered her. She said, "I have to stay in a crowd; I cannot be alone."

We all make mistakes. One cannot fix the past—spilled milk cannot be put back into the bottle. Once you repent and God forgives you, move on! You cannot go backward and forward at the same time. Try not to make the same mistake again, and forgive yourself. "And Jesus said unto him, No man, having put his hand to the plough, and looking back, is fit for the kingdom of God" (Luke 9:62).

King David had regrets about an adulterous affair and conspiring to have a man killed. God forgave him, and the Bible states that King David was a man after God's own heart. I can understand why God loved him so much. King David endangered his life for his Father's sheep—he even fought a bear and a lion to rescue one of his Father's lambs. God looks at the heart. However, God did not remove the consequences of King David's actions: "Remember not the sins of my youth" (Psalm 25:7).

We are given one earthly house. One can abuse one's body and mind, but another will not be given in this life. And trying to ease one's pain with a substance only adds problems. Eventually, one has to sober up! The body of Christ must teach that one cannot work, sleep, or drink problems away. One has to live with one's conscience. However, one can put those burdens where they rightfully belong by giving them to Jesus. God, in his Word, says he never slumbers: "he that keepeth thee will not slumber. Behold, he that keepeth Israel shall neither slumber nor sleep" (Psalm 121:2–4). I, on the other hand, need my rest. There's no need for both of us to stay up all night, so I put my burdens on God's shoulders, where they rightfully belong. "It is vain for you to rise up early, to sit up late, to eat the bread of sorrows; for so he giveth his beloved sleep" (Psalm 27:2). And God is the only one that can do something about our problems.

Don't let your children drive you crazy. You are just a steward. Your children belong to God anyway: "Lo, children are an heritage of the Lord: and the fruit of the womb is his reward" (Psalm 127:3). So give them back to him and say, "More power to you. I have my own problems." Think about it! Why let something or somebody that is not yours to start with send you to an early grave? Sleep; get your rest. Life is short. Do not let God dump your children on you—give them back! And that is the Word of God.

Another point that I want to make on wholeness is that human nature is basically the same regardless of where one goes. Many change jobs because of conflict with their boss or other employees, but life has taught me that the true solution is learning how to cope with human nature. Human nature is the same no matter where one goes. Jealousy, meanness, prejudice, and so on are part of life. If you change jobs for another reason, like to get a better salary or because you dislike the work, that is different. Just be certain that God is leading you to change. Work is work, and people are people. Whenever you change jobs, you have to learn the new job, learn how to work with a new group of people, and so on. That can be stressful. Sometimes it is better to stay with the devil that you know.

My dad used to say that you have to leave some people alone—speak and then keep moving. As long as there is no malice or hatred in your heart, that kind of behavior is a way of getting along with others. The Bible tells us that if you want a friend, you should first show yourself friendly: "A man that hath friends must shew himself friendly" (Proverbs 18:24). I can truly say that there is no hatred or malice in my heart, and I do try to get along with everyone. Personally speaking, I enjoy my own company and like the person that I have become. I enjoy me! I am sincere but plainspoken. I can respect those who cannot accept my personality, but I will not change to fit into someone else's mold. I'm sorry! I am happy, and I am happy with Jesus alone.

Lust destroys the flesh: "For he that soweth to his flesh shall of the flesh reap corruption" (Galatians 6:8). The sin in our flesh is powerful; it takes the Holy Spirit and godly discipline to bring our flesh into subjection. That is the danger of playing with temptation—flesh will win. A disciplined mind stays away from the things that can overpower the flesh and the things that the flesh is weak to. The consequences of fleshly lust are diseases, guilt, a bad reputation, no peace or happiness, and a broken fellowship with God.

The Holy Spirit wants Christians to have a good quality of life, and that is why these things are written. God wants us to enjoy life and to have fun in the right way. It is difficult to enjoy life when one has many regrets. The same peace that the world offers to help people forget their problems and the same state of euphoria that can be temporarily found in substance abuse—like drinking alcohol, taking drugs, or smoking weed—can be found in Christ Jesus, but one has to live a disciplined life to receive such peace and euphoria.

The Bible tells us, "Love not the world, neither the things that are in the world. For all that is in the world, the lust of the flesh, and the lust of the eyes, and the pride of life, is not of the Father but is of the world" (1 John 2:15–16). All that the world has to offer is "the lust of the flesh, and the lust of the eyes, and the pride of life." That is it! And those three things will cause one a lot of heartache and sorrow in life.

One cannot purchase everything desired. Credit cards have to paid off. I talk to a lot of people, and I once struck up a conversation with a man who was doing repair work in my apartment. He told me that he'd bought a new house, furnished it completely, and purchased a new car, all at the same time. The lesson that he'd learned was you can't have "it all" in this life. He said debt had cost him many a sleepless nights. Hiding from bill collectors is *stressful*!

Many churches teach the gospel stories, but are we teaching our youth that God has a code of ethics? Teaching them this is part of my vision for the body of Christ. When our youth go out into the world, God will let them suffer the consequences of their own actions. Whatever happens to them will happen, including prison and death. As long as we as the body of Christ have properly taught them about God's code of ethics and given them full knowledge of the consequences of their actions, we will not have blood or guilt on our hands. We will eliminate the blame game and place the responsibility squarely on their individual shoulders.

Luke 12:47–48 says, "And the servant, which knew his lord's will, and prepared not himself, neither did according to his will, shall be beaten with many stripes. But he that knew not, and did commit things worthy of stripes, shall be beaten with few stripes." However, no one has an excuse, because the laws of God are written on the table of the heart. Many doing wrong know better! When our youth know the truth, God may not spare them to live long lives. However, it is better that we as the body of Christ know that our youth knew the truth rather than wishing we had taught them better. God will not let us grieve heavily when we have done out duty. "Be not over much wicked, neither be thou foolish: why shouldest thou die before thy time?" (Ecclesiastes 7:17). Wholeness doctrine lets us know that, according to God's Word, which is true, "whatsoever one soweth, that shall he also reap" (Galatians 6:7). God is not going to put someone else—a parent, a pastor, or so on—in the bed that one has made up for oneself. The bed that one makes for oneself in life is the bed that one will sleep in.

My last point in teaching wholeness is regarding marriage. I have attended many churches that strongly focus on marriage—the utopia of life. Marriage is wonderful—it means not going through life alone. However, regardless of how beautiful a marriage may be, it is not guaranteed to last a lifetime, because a mate may pass on and leave one alone. Approximately forty or more years ago, I met a woman at the DMV who was trying to purchase tags for her car. She told me that she'd had a wonderful husband who had passed away. She had never been employed outside the home, and he had been a good provider. After his death, she'd had to pick up the pieces. She'd known nothing about what it cost to live or how to pay bills and handle financial matters. She'd realized only after his death that, not knowing any better and not understanding the cost of living, she had been asking him for things that he really could not afford to give her. At an older age, she'd had to learn how to pay bills and do all the things her husband had done. She told me, "Don't let anybody do you like that—get out and learn." I've known many who were in happy marriages but who are alone today because their spouse has passed on. I read a book years ago about women whose spouses had passed away and the subsequent problems they encountered. Some had to move in with their children, and some had regrets about doing so because they were used as maids and babysitters.

My point is, if God decides not to give you a mate or companionship, he knows best. Years from now, you will look back and see that marriage is a temporary state; it is of this world only. Many that are happily married today may end up alone in the end. The beauty of the single life is that you learn to stand on your own two feet. You aren't dependent upon another for survival, and that is a good feeling. You are whole!

Adam and Eve—man and woman—were created to provide each other companionship and to replenish the earth. Matthew 22:30 says, "For in the resurrection they neither marry, nor are given in marriage, but are as the angels of God in heaven." Single life is the highest calling, but not many can attain it. Young people should know that one cannot have marriage and freedom. One has to choose. In marriage, one is subject to another person, and God has ordained order in the home. Marriage can be confining, but love is what keeps two people together a lifetime. If and when one truly loves, subjection is not a burden.

True love is blinding. For example, while others can easily see the faults of our children, many of us are blinded to those faults because of the love that we have for our children. Perhaps you've had a child come over to visit before and found that he or she got on your nerves more quickly than your own child. This often happens because we don't have the same kind of love for others' children as we do for our own. Many children would be much better off if their parents let them suffer the consequences of their actions, but that is sometimes difficult for parents because of their love. God's love is different. Those he loves he chastises.

One needs to choose one's romantic partners carefully. According to the news, this year alone, several women have lost their lives in relationships. My dad taught young women that you can't always get rid of the person that you get involved with. He would say, "Some men will come down the chimney and get you."

Marriage is not for everyone, and it can be challenging. Marriage vows are taken before God, and God holds us accountable. We all make mistakes in life—I did! However, not everyone is given a second chance. Sometimes, as in my case, one is unequally yoked, and God may lead one out of a marriage. Before leaving a marriage, one has to make sure that that is the perfect will of God. God does not set us free simply to lead promiscuous lives. Young people should be taught that marriage is a major step in life. Divorce is also a major step. Only God and the Holy Spirit can lead in such serious endeavors.

Ministries

No one has to argue over ministries today. With the world crumbling around us, everyone can find something to do for Christ. Nursing homes always need volunteers to help seniors with their activities. When I volunteered in a nursing home, I would help with bingo boards, sing, and just visit. Members of different churches would come during the week to visit as well. Having volunteered myself, I can say with certainty that it is a rewarding experience. This is a work that any in the body of Christ can do, individually and collectively. One of the residents whom I visited once told me that members of her home church had come to visit her during her first year of stay but had stopped coming. One simply has to sign up and get permission from the nursing home to volunteer, and then one can help brighten the days of the residents."

We have schools that desperately need help as well. Parents could help with children during the lunch break, and seniors, with the school's and God's permission, could sit in on classrooms and help with the little ones. When the kids are disorderly, these volunteers could give them hugs; our children need nurturing. It is sad to say, but schools are suspending second graders nowadays. It is impossible for one young teacher to handle twenty-five to thirty of today's children. The two grandchildren that I help with are a challenge, and I need help sometimes. If I could discipline the old-school way, things would work out much better.

Some ministries need collective effort. For example, ministering to prisoners would be better if done collectively and with leadership. Such ministering would probably require special permission that would only be given to a collective body.

My vision is to put all the church folks to work—get them out there! I met a very intelligent young man many years ago who told me that he was from a large family. His dad owned several gas stations. He said his father would not buy him and his siblings clothing or give them spending money when they were growing up. However, he had offered them jobs, and the money they'd earned had been theirs to keep. That is wisdom! And when I met this young man, he had a fancy car and was a businessman. His dad had taught him something.

One day my granddaughter had a note in her backpack stating that an after-school activity for elementary school children was going to be canceled because they could not find volunteers. How tragic! Where is the body of Christ? The Bible tells us that the harvest is plentiful but the laborers are few. One of my granddaughters got very upset with me when

I told her that she was all month and no action. "This people draweth nigh unto me with their month, and honoureth me with their lips but their heart is far from me" (Matthew 15:8). I could be wrong, but I think that this granddaughter is in school today just to prove a point. In any case, I love her dearly.

Where are the millions of church folk? No one has to be burdened. We have enough members in the body of Christ to do shifts—a few hours here and there!

The Bible tells us that wisdom is with the ancient: "With the ancient is wisdom: and in length of days understanding" (Job 12:12). It takes time and experience to be seasoned—to have wisdom. All that wisdom and experience playing bingo and dominos all day! I am not passing judgment on these beautiful programs set up for our seniors. Such programs do good work and have their place. But what a waste of wisdom! Those seniors are needed in school classrooms and lunchrooms. The young teachers have not lived long enough to have the wisdom needed. They have academic knowledge but lack old-school wisdom. The philosopher Montaigne once said, "I speak the truth, not as much as I would, but as much as I dare; and I dare a little the more as I get older."

The problem is that we have turned our society as a whole over to the youth. They have the academic learning and technical skills but lack the knowledge and wisdom that comes with age and experience. In our country age is not honored, but the Bible tells us that it should be: "The hoary [white or gray] head is a crown of glory. if it be found in the way of righteousness" (Proverbs 16:31). "The glory of young men is their strength: and the beauty of old men is the grey head" (Psalm 20:29). Many seniors who are of sound mind would possibly enjoy doing something constructive for Christ. Give them a small stipend to help supplement their income and provide transportation. Seniors could have small classes and teach our girls to sew and cook, to respect their bodies, and so on, and teach godliness at the same time. Let it be a fun environment while teaching. Let the spirit of God lead. This is just my vision for the church. These things may never happen, but I can dream! After all, the church is not the building; it's the people.

Programs set up outside of the church are expensive, and they do not have a godly environment. Plant spiritual seeds! The world has set up its programs; the body of Christ, individually and collectively, needs to set up godly programs that let our youth learn godliness while having fun. Let young people write their own plays, and open the doors to empty churches for youth activity. Close the churches some Sunday mornings and have church at the park, at a nursing home, in a shelter, or so on, if the Holy Spirit so leads. These things take money, effort, and volunteers. We have churches practically on every block, and my vision is to put them to work.

Take the message to the world! Don't wait for the world to come to you. We sing and preach to the same folk week after week. Is the heart any better after the service's close? If the answer is yes, then how did we lose a generation of young people? That is my question, and that is my dilemma. I want to rock the boat here.

Many pastors know that people burn out with the same old problems. My dad was a pastor, and he let life stress him out. How many are really looking for a solution to problems? I am not trying to be facetious, but fifty years from now, many will still be walking around with the same problems. I watched my dad pastor and saw the stress that he was under. One has to make decisions in life. That takes godly strength. And if one is living in a stressful situation, there is only once decision to be made—either accept the situation or move on. Only the individual involved can make that decision. It's said that only the strong survive, but one cannot become strong unless the truth is told: "And ye shall know the truth, and the truth shall make you free" (John 9:32).

People have many reasons for not attending church services. One reason is that it costs money to go to church, and another reason is that, at least in my experience, many church folk are not friendly. However, if one has accepted Jesus Christ as Lord and savior, all is well. Some may feel guilty for not having money to give or proper clothing to wear, but these things don't matter. Church is in the heart: "Neither shall they say, Lo here! Or lo there! For, behold, the kingdom of God is within you" (Luke 17:21).

Many saints have been stumbling blocks because of the life lived in front of the ungodly: "But take heed lest by any means this liberty of yours become a stumblingblock to them that are weak" (1 Corinthians 8:9). Christians are chastised for wrongdoing and in the end will have eternal life, but the nonbeliever will be lost in the end. My dad often told a story about a boy and his dog. The little boy was dragging his dog home, and someone stopped him and asked him why he was dragging his dog. He said, "Mister, I am trying to get him home, but since he won't follow, I am going to drag him home." God has to do the same thing sometimes—drag us home. Father Time will sit you down, and Mother Nature will shut you down. Sometimes "life" brings us back to God and not our goodness and righteousness; it is because high blood pressure, diabetes, dialysis, heart problems, back problems, and arthritis, etc. will not allow the human body to do the things that the flesh desires!

Many are singing, "Use me, Lord." God can use you, even if there is no light in your life, even if you are salt that has lost its savor because of ungodly living? All is not lost! God can still use you. You can give money to youth programs and help financially!

Each of us can start our own individual ministry. *Pray first and get God's permission, and then take action.* You could take a few hot dogs to the park, hang out a sign saying "Free Food," and wait. There will not be room enough to receive! Play inspirational Christian music that feeds the soul—I am personally a lover of hymns—and extend the invitation to Christ. Tell people to ask God to lead them to a church, and let God take it from there.

One of the problems from my perspective is doctrine. I visited a church many years ago, and the pastor basically said that those who did not speak in tongues would not be able to sing in the choir. That is confusing—let people be saved. Time is winding up! If one accepts Jesus Christ as Lord and savior, one has eternal life. Don't confuse people. Jesus is the password to the kingdom—that's it! As mentioned earlier, I am plainspoken. Therefore, I am saying to the collective body of Christ—*keep it simple!* Young people would say "keep it real."

> If when you give the best of your service,
> Telling the world that the Savior is come;
> Be not dismayed when men don't believe you;
> He'll understand and say, "Well done."
>
> —Lucie E. Campbell,
> <u>"He'll Understand and Say 'Well Done'"</u>

> Great men are not always wise: neither do the aged understand judgment.
>
> —Job 32:9

Religion

If religion could save,
Very few would be lost.
Bu religion can't do it.
Salvation is in the name of Jesus.
It was purchased at Calvary's cross.
We fill the churches on Sunday mornings
Wearing our best clothes,
But is the heart any better
After the service's close?

We sing, dance, shout, and praise him;
We make a lot of noise.
But is God really in it?
Did we hear his voice?
Jesus is seldom in high places.
He's difficult to find in a crowd.
Seldom does he get invited
On Sunday mornings,
Usually because he doesn't
Wear the right clothes.

The Buck Stops Here

But we've got our religion.
We take it everywhere we go.
Don't call us on Sunday morning—
We go to church, you know.
But when we get to heaven,
Will Jesus tell us to depart?
We'll tell him we have good religion,
But he'll say, "Depart.
I know you not."

It will be difficult To believe him.
All that religion you know—
But he will tell us in the end
That religion is just a show!

> For the wrath of God is revealed from heaven against all ungodliness and unrighteousness of men, who hold the truth in unrighteousness.
>
> —Romans 1:18

The Spiritual Body in Disarray
The head dislikes the hands and feet—they just don't
Agree! No movement.
The ears dislike the eyes—they are different colors.
No vision—can't hear God speaking.
The tongue wants to speak, but the mouth refuses to
Open—can't be fed—spiritually dead.

The bowels refuse to move because they don't like what
they were fed—body perishes.
The heart refuses to pump blood to a portion of the brain—
The body is handicapped.
The other organs wanted to work, but the heart didn't
Like their faces!

5

Love

The greatest definition of love that I have ever read is found in 1 Corinthians 13:1–13, which reads in part, "Though I speak with the tongue of men and of angels, and have not charity, I am become as sounding brass, or a tinkling cymbal. And though I have the gift of prophecy, and understand all mysteries, and all knowledge; and though I have all faith, so that I could remove mountains, and have not charity … it profiteth me nothing … And now abideth faith, hope, charity [love], these three; but the greatest of these is charity" (1 Corinthians 13:1–3, 13:13).

Love is the greatest gift! Why is love the greatest gift? Because love never dies. Many years ago, I read in a love column that you can kill love, but love never dies. A person badly mistreated by someone that they love can lose or overcome the earthly love that they once had for the individual. Many loved ones who have left the earth are still present with us today, alive in the hearts of those who loved them and in their work, which continues to influence people. Such people—like Jesus Christ, Martin Luther King Jr., parents and grandparents, hymn writers, poets, writers, and so on—are still effective today. The Bible tells us that our individual testimonies will not be heard until our deceases: "For where a testament is, there must also of necessity be the death of the testator. For a testament is of force after men are dead: otherwise, it is of no strength at all while the testator liveth" (Hebrews 9:16–17). Without drinking water, all would perish within days—the entire world! That is how valuable water is. How many of us can fully appreciate its value? It is difficult to appreciate it because it is plentiful in our great nation. We appreciate things most when they are gone. In fact, I read in a book that Martin Luther King Jr. was more effective in death than in life. The message that he tried to convey for approximately twelve years was heard around the world in twelve minutes after his death.

The love that Jesus showed for the world by giving his life will never die. Even though he is greatly rejected by many, his power, his love, his anointing, and his influence will never and can never be destroyed. God's power, his presence for those in Christ, can be felt. He lives. And the wonderful part is that we can't die. A spirit cannot be killed. That is why God told us not to fear those who can kill the body, because the soul—the real you—cannot die. One just changes houses. One's spirit, testimony, preached message, and planted seeds will still be here on earth, living in someone's heart. Many contrary children, who would not listen while their parents were living, straighten up and live by their parents' teachings after their parents die. That is the importance of teaching and training our children and our youth; they will come back to the teaching if they have been taught. That is God's promise to us!

I often keep Bible tracts with me. Years ago, while walking to church, I would walk past a corner where drugs were being sold. I would often stop and talk to the young men and leave them with a Bible tract. I could always tell the young men who had been trained correctly because when they saw me coming, they would run and hide or at least hide their alcohol. They did this because of respect for God—godly respect. It was not because of me but because of the God in me, which they saw because at some point in their lives they had been taught godly respect. Young people who have never had godly training act differently. There is a coldness about them and a danger. I could always tell the difference. I told these young people, "I am just another human being. Why hide from me when God sees the wrong that you are doing?"

One could symbolically compare love to water and hate to dirt. Both water and dirt have a destructive nature, but water is more powerful. Water can seep through the smallest crack. Similarly, love can touch all. Dirt—hate—cannot. Water is soothing—a hot tub cleans, and hot coffee and tea comforts—and we cannot survive without it. Love acts the same way—it comforts, it cares, it can help one to heal, and if missing in a child's life, it has lifelong effects. Plants can also take root in water. Dirt can't do what water can do, and neither can hate do what love can. Does one ever want to be around dirt—hatred? Someone who was involved in the situation and who is now deceased once told me a story about a child who, decades ago, was taken back and forth to the hospital for various reasons. Finally, after sitting on the floor and playing with the child, a doctor diagnosed the child as having never felt love and having been left in the crib most of the time. According to the person who took the child, the child recuperated and ended up okay. Love is powerful.

As comforting as water can be, it can destroy—drown, corrode, cause rust, and so on. Water is more damaging than dirt. If someone dumps a ton of dirt into a home, it can be shoveled out. But if a ton of water comes in, it will destroy some things and cause severe damage. We, as the body of Christ, can throw some love on haters—we can love, in spite of. Love is more powerful than hate!

As human beings, we are all connected: "And hath made of one blood all nations of men for to dwell on all the face of the earth" (Acts 17:26). We have different features, cultures, and lifestyles, but all humans are the same. All human bodies function the same way. Babies, for example, all go through the same stages of development. All people are birthed into the world, and all leave the same way. And whether accepted or rejected, all will wake up on the other side. We are all connected! One race—the human race.

Hatred comes from one's environment, from being taught incorrectly. Hatred can also come from unfair treatment or other personal reasons. One may have a justified reason for hatred, but God, in his infinite wisdom, has commanded us to forgive and to love. Forgiveness and love are better for one's health. The sad part about hatred is that it destroys the hater, not the person or object hated. Hatred makes one miserable!

The real hater is not always the person that the hate is manifested through or the one who pulls the trigger. The real hater is the person who sows the seed of discord: "These six things doth the lord hate: Yea, seven are an abomination unto him: A proud look, a lying tongue, and hands that shed innocent blood … and he that soweth discord among brethren" (Proverbs 6:16–19).

Our great nation is slowly crumbling. What are we, as followers of Christ, doing about the hatred that is rapidly dividing this great nation? How can we exemplify love? If the situation is ever going to get fixed, we, as the collective body of Christ, will have to do it. The politicians cannot fix the situation. Why would one spend billions to win an election that pays far, far less in salary? Politics and religion don't mix. We, as the collective body of Christ, can rise and help our great nation heal! The world is watching. The politicians and elected officials cannot heal the nation, but we, the collective body of Christ, have the power to make the difference! "Not by might, nor by power, but by my spirit, saith the Lord of Hosts" (Zechariah 4:6).

When there is a fire, the fire department does not throw dirt on the building; they use water to put the fire out. Similarly, we can, collectively, love the hell out of people. Fixing the world has to be done God's way, through teaching. An eye for an eye causes blindness. And with the tit-for-tat approach, there is no end to the fighting. "Ye have heard that it hath been said, Thou shalt love thy neighbor, and hate thine enemy. But I say unto you, Love your enemies, Bless them that curse you, do good to them that hate you … for [God] maketh his sun to rise on the evil and on the good, and sendeth rain on the just and the unjust" (Matthew 5:43–45). God does not retaliate. God knows that a judgment day is coming. That's love!

We all know that certain races of people have endured and still face unjust treatment—the black-white struggle. However, if the hatred, destructive behaviors, and violence continues, we will all suffer. For the good of the nation, someone needs to have good sense! Come to the table for discussion. We all hurt the same way. Dialogue is what is needed. "Wisdom is better than weapons of war" (Ecclesiastes 9:18).

Slavery was terrible, but we do not have the facts as to how or why slavery came about. We have been told certain things, but God and only God knows the truth. History gets distorted. In Old Testament times, the Israelites, God's people, were sold in and out of bondage for disobedience. In contrast, Jacob's youngest son, Joseph, was sold into bondage by his brothers because of jealousy. They did it for evil, but God allowed it for divine purpose. My point here is that the hatred that blacks have for whites and that whites have for blacks might have been divinely orchestrated. Slavery was ugly and painful, but it would be wonderful if we could let the past go. "Forgive, and ye shall be forgiven" (Luke 6:37). Let's move forward! I have read many books in my lifetime, and from reading, I know that things could have happened differently. Joseph was sold by his own brothers. He was lied on and imprisoned while in bondage, but God was always with him, and he was blessed while in captivity. There was money involved in the slave trade. God alone knows the truth. All this hatred could possibly be misdirected. So let's leave it alone! Let's wait until we get to heaven and learn the truth.

In the meantime, the struggle continues, but hatred and violence are the wrong approach. They cause loss of innocent lives and unnecessary suffering. Hatred is destructive and does not solve problems. We, as the collective body of Christ, can take a stand for righteousness—God's way. Violence is not the answer—godly love is. Love conquers all! The struggle never ends. There is an old Negro spiritual with the lyrics "I'm going to lay down my sword and spear, down by the riverside." That is spiritual warfare—good versus evil, justice versus injustice, nonviolence versus violence. The struggle never ends, but our weapons are not carnal! "Put on the whole armour of God, that you may be able to stand against the wiles of the devil" (Ephesians 6:11).

Lastly, we must forgive. Jesus was unmercifully beaten, spit upon, and then crucified—cruel treatment. And he was innocent. Man's inhumanity to man! Yet he forgave: "Then Jesus said, Father, forgive them; for they know not what they do" (Luke 23:34). That is unconditional love. Joseph forgave his brethren as well. "And he said, I am Joseph, your brother, whom ye sold into Egypt. Now therefore be not grieved, nor angry with yourselves, that you sold me hither: for God did send me before you to preserve life" (Genesis 45:4–5). If Joseph can forgive his brethren for selling him into slavery and indirectly causing him to be imprisoned and suffer much grief, we can forgive also and heal as a people, as a nation, and as God's representatives on the earth. "Forgive, and ye shall be forgiven" (Luke 6:37)!

FORSAKEN
When we are forsaken by love ones,
Those we call our own,
We can look at God's Word and see,
That we are not alone.

For Joseph was sold by his brethren,
Those he called his own.
But God had already prepared for him
Another home.

Jesus was forsaken by those he loved,
Those he called his own.
But Oh! What God had in store for him!
When he arrived home!
(Let your conversation be without covetousness; and
Be content with such things as ye have; for he hath said,
I will never leave thee, nor forsake thee (Hebrews 13:5).

Getting Ahead
People are fighting and killing,
Trying to get ahead,
Not realizing that a hundred years from now,
Most will be dead.
And when we enter that great beyond,
We're going to be judged
For all the things we have done.

Claudia Harris

Many tears will be shed,
But it will be too late,
Because God is giving us a chance now T
o avoid that fate.

> For I have no pleasure in the death of him that dieth,
> said the Lord God; wherefore, turn yourselves, and live.
>
> —Ezekiel 18:32

6

Death

Spiritual Death
Christians can die spiritually. Adam, the first man created after God's own image, died a spiritual death—a broken fellowship with God—because of disobedience. The body of Christ, individually and collectively, can also die spiritually. We can lose our influence and effectiveness as lights in the world. We are the light of the world and the salt of the earth. We need God's power, individually and collectively, to do God's work. One may have outlets, lightbulbs, electrical cords, and all the necessary equipment, but if the power company shuts off the power, when one flips the switch on, the lights will remain off because there is *no power*. The body operates symbolically in the same way. When the brain dies, one is brain-dead. Even though there is breath in the body, the body is useless. The life-support machine is disconnected, with permission, because the body is nonfunctional. Matthew 5:13–14 says, "Ye are the salt of the earth: but if the salt have lost his savour, wherewith shall it be salted? It is thenceforth good for nothing, but to be cast out, and to be trodden under foot of men. Ye are the light of the world. A city that is set on a hill cannot be hid."

The church has been given the power. If change comes about in our nation, it will not come from the White House, where many are trying to go. Politics and religion do not mix. Healing for our nation will come when we individually and collectively as a body of born-again believers take a peaceful stand for righteousness. Zechariah 4:6 says, "Not by might, nor by power, but by my spirit, saith the Lord of hosts." We, individually and collectively, have the power of change—the power to enlighten and change the mind-sets of those who have been taught wrong and those who are doing wrong. We can point people in a more positive direction. We are all connected, so if the nation goes down, we all go down together.

Many women live in abusive relationships and refuse to get help or to leave the relationship. God is long-suffering, good, kind, and merciful. However, God will not live in an abusive relationship. He gives us a chance. The Holy Spirit will warn, correct, lead, and guide, but the Holy Spirit will not continue to strive with an individual when that individual continually rejects him. The Holy Spirit will silence himself, and one can be turned over to a reprobate mind—rejected. God does not need us; we need him. "I also will laugh at your calamity; I will mock when your fear cometh; When your fear cometh as desolation, and your destruction cometh as a whirlwind; when distress and anguish cometh upon you; Then shall they call upon me, but I will not answer" (Proverbs 1:26–28). Many of us want to treat God like some of our loved ones treat us. They call or come in a time of need, but once their need is met, they vanish until they have another need—back and forth, in and out.

Adam was kicked out of the Garden of Eden permanently. I am sure that he had regrets, but his plight changed. Sin entered into the world because of his disobedience. You may ask, "How will I know if the Holy Spirit has silenced himself?" You will know because your conscience will no longer convict; evil will appear to be good, and good will appear to be evil. Your conscience will no longer bother you. That is a dangerous place to be with God.

I mentioned earlier that I have been in the harvest a lifetime and have heard many stories. One such story came to me from a "backsliding Christian"— her words. She said the devil tried to make her kill her husband. They were driving, and when he stopped at a stop sign, she pulled a pistol out of her purse. When he saw the gun, he jumped out of the car and ran zigzag down an alley. She couldn't shoot him, because he would not stand still. She told me, "When a person sells out to the devil, it is difficult to get back." She, along with her children, attempted to go to church a few Sundays, but it soon ended. A man in a drug treatment program told me a similar story. He had recently given his life to Christ, and I assume that he thought that he was going to be delivered from his ungodly lifestyle overnight. He was almost in tears while speaking with me. He said he wanted to do the right thing but would always find himself back to his original state.

Sin is similar to weight gain. The weight was not gained overnight, and it will not be lost overnight. Turning one's life around or walking in newness of life takes time; it is a process, and one must remain headed in the right direction. My dad used to say, "You can lose a battle and still win the war." Keep trying. Don't quit! The race is not given to the swift nor to the strong but to the one who endures to the end. And just like when losing a large amount of weight, the flabby skin will not disappear on its own. And I have heard it said on cable TV that the hanging skin is almost as bad as the weight.

Some are never able to take the weight off, even though they make a sincere effort to do so. Similarly, one can successfully stop taking drugs, but the desire may never leave, and one can relapse. A recovering addict told me that one has to change one's environment to overcome. Guess what! One may never totally overcome an addiction; God is looking at the heart and the mind—that *perfect will* to overcome. King David was forgiven for committing adultery and murder, and the Bible tells us that his heart was perfect toward God. Listening to the flesh, or temptation, can get one in a lot of trouble. A higher court can overrule decisions made by a lower court. One can let the higher court, the mind, rule over the flesh. This is what it means to have self-control and be disciplined. First John 4:4 says, "Ye are of God little children, and have overcome them: because greater is he that is in you, than he that is in the world." While passing out Bible tracts, I met a man who cried like a baby and asked me to pray for him because he wanted to be delivered from drugs. That is why it is so important to teach our youth and continually warn them about the consequences of bad choices.

Street ministry can be dangerous. That is the reason one must be led by the Holy Spirit before attempting to do this type of ministry. A young man approached me many years ago when I was passing out Bible tracts and said that I reminded him of his sister. He was pleasant and cordial; however, someone standing across the street called me over and told me that he was a rapist and that as soon as he got me near an alley, he was going to rape me. God will protect you if he sends you, but do not attempt street ministry on your own.

The law of the harvest applies to everything in one's life: "Be not deceived; God is not mocked: for whatsoever a man soweth, that shall he also reap. For he that soweth to his flesh shall of the flesh reap corruption" (Galatians 6:7–8). If one wants good grades in school, one must study— the law of the harvest. I enjoy food—love it! However, I do not want to gain excess weight. I have more energy and feel better when I exercise and eat healthful food. Therefore, I deny my flesh certain foods that it craves. Everything that seems good to you is not good for you. Again, this is the law of the harvest—what you sow you reap. Plant corn, and corn comes up. One cannot plant corn and look for tomatoes. Many may say that life is tough, but life is what you make it. And a broken fellowship with God is not easily restored.

There is an old saying "An idle mind is the devil's workshop." Personally, I try to fill my life with positive activity by reading, going to the gym, going to the library, going for walks, enjoying nature, doing volunteer work, and so on, and nearly all these things are free. Otherwise, I sit around and nibble on unhealthful food, watch television, and generally waste my time on earth. For me, gossiping on the telephone is also a waste of God's precious time. And if I lie in bed too long, I don't have energy. I stay actively involved because I feel better when I do.

Collectively and individually, we have a great work ahead of us. We have lost a generation of youth. This is not the time for division. We are all connected. "Thus said the Lord God unto these bones; Behold, I will cause breath to enter into you and ye shall live … So I prophesied as I was commanded: and as I prophesied, there was a noise, and behold a shaking, and the bones came together, bone to his bone" (Ezekiel 37:5–7).

Earthly Death

Death comes to all—the believer and the unbeliever. One may argue, fight, and refute the Word of God, but no one escapes death. My dad used to say that we all have "an unbreakable appointment with death." Ecclesiastes 3:1–2 says, "To everything there is a season … A time to be born, and a time to die," and Ecclesiastes 8:8 says, "There is no man that hath power over the spirit to retain the spirit; neither hath he power in the day of death; and there is no discharge in that war."

There are those who believe that this life is the end and that there is no hereafter. Some do not believe in God at all, but that is a God-given choice. We are free to choose. "And if any man hear my words, and believe not, I judge him not; for I came not to judge the world, but to save the world. He that rejecteth me, and receiveth not my words, hath one that judgeth him: the word that I have spoken, the same shall judge him in the last day" (John 12:47–48). I am not trying to force Christianity on those who believe differently, but I would ask that you carefully reference the above scriptures and a few more later on and ask yourself, "Is there any truth in them?" Many people believe that there is someone or something greater but do not accept Jesus Christ as the savior of the world. That also is one's right, one's choice.

God is the great provider. He provides for all—the believer and the unbeliever. God feeds all because without seeds, the sun, and the rain, there would be no food, and all would die of starvation and thirst—the rich and the poor. "Moreover the profit of the earth is for all: the king himself is served by the field" (Ecclesiastes 5:9). We breathe God's air. Even though the oxygen we breathe and the wind that blows cannot be seen, everyone knows that they are there. We are all dependent on God, whether we acknowledge it or not. God has the upper hand—the power over all. There is no argument. Psalm 14:1 says, "The fool hath said in his heart, There is no God."

Sometimes when I correct my grandchild, she will say to me, "I hate you." That doesn't bother me, because I know that she is a child and that I am providing for her and supplying her basic needs. It would be foolish for me to argue with a child that is immature and does not understand.

God is not upset because of rejection. Why? Because we all come from God and we all go back to God; there is no argument. "For whether we live, we live unto the Lord: whether we live therefore, or die, we are the Lord's" (Romans 14:8).

Unbelievers

Many do not believe in the Bible,
Claiming it is a book that is not true,
One that is written by other people,
Everyday people just like me and you.

But God does not force his Word upon us—
The right to choose is solely left to you.
He never forces one to accept him—
That choice is left entirely to you.

But God has commissioned some to tell you
That even though you don't believe his Word,
Jesus was sent down to earth to save you.
I am sure that you have already heard.

Although you do not believe the Bible
Or that Jesus Christ came to save the world,
You will still see Jesus when you leave here.
Now, does that sound to you to be absurd?

Those who do not believe in the Bible,
Still have to answer to death's beck and call.
Whether you believe the Bible or not,
You will still leave earth and answer for all!

There are many religions that believe in God but do not believe that Jesus is the password to the kingdom. And that belief also is a choice. I am a born-again believer in the birth, life, death, and resurrection of Jesus

Christ. I believe that salvation is in the name of Jesus, and I will leave the earth believing that Jesus is the Son of God.

Whatever decision you choose to make, please make it now, because once you cross over, it is too late, and no one knows when his or her time is up. Whether one believes in the Bible or not, Bible prophecy is unfolding and clearly visible to the human eye. If one studies the book of Revelation, one will realize all the Bible prophecies that are coming true today. The earth is getting hotter and hotter, children are killing their parents, there is ungodly living as in the days of Noah, families are divided, some people have been cast into prison, and the name of Jesus has been taken out of the workplace. I even believe that the Antichrist has come, as I believe the Antichrist is just a spirit that is against Jesus. We have been living in the last days for two thousand years: "Little children, it is the last time: and as ye have heard that antichrist shall come, even now, there are many antichrists; whereby we know that it is the last time" (1 John 2:18). We know that God's time is not our time, because God's Word tells us that one day with God is as a thousand years and a thousand years as one day. My point here is that no one can deny or dispute the above prophecies, because everyone can see these things happening.

If the above is true, than according to the Bible, there is a lot of suffering prophesied ahead—the great tribulation, food shortages, lack of drinking water, and more. Growing food is going to be a problem with the great heat that has been prophesied, as the sun will dry up the earth. One may have money to buy food; however, the food may not be available. The great tribulation is not something that I want to go through!

According to God's Word, the saints, those in the body of Christ, will leave the earth—the rapture of the church. That is what we are looking forward to—the next great event to come upon the earth. "Then shall two be in the field; the one shall be taken, and the other left. Two women shall be grinding at the mill; the one shall be taken and the other left" (Matthew 24:40–41). I recommend reading the entire chapter of Matthew 24 to learn more about the end-time. The rapture is suppose to be quick—instant: "In a moment, in the twinkling of an eye, at the last trump; for the trumpet shall sound and the dead shall be raised incorruptible and we shall be changed" (1 Corinthians 15:52). There will be no time to get ready or to make a decision for Christ. Before one can blink an eye, the body of Christ will leave the earth.

Now is the hour of decision because tomorrow is not promised. Do not play with your soul. Salvation is a life-or-death decision. Everyone leaves the earth. Where will you spend eternity? "But without faith it is impossible to please him, for he that cometh to God must believe that he is, and that he is a rewarder to them that diligently seek him" (Hebrews 11:6). The sad part about investing all in this life is that you can't take it with you. Everything remains. It all ends at the grave: "For we brought nothing into this world and it is certain that we can carry nothing out" (1 Timothy 6:7). "Then shall the dust return to the earth as it was: and the spirit return unto God who gave it" (Ecclesiastes 12:7).

> For what is a man profited, if he shall gain the whole world, and lose his own soul?
>
> —Matthew 16:26

> And though after my skin worms destroy this body, yet in my flesh shall I see God.
>
> —Job 19:26

One day soon we shall hear the last words, "It is finished."—your life and mine. The Scribe of years will have placed the last period after the last word and blotted the page. What is written will remain an indelible record. No year, month, day, hour or minute can be recalled and relived. Regrets will be futile; sighs and sobs that will echo through the dark caverns of a hopeless tomorrow. We shall be stripped of everything save character. We shall carry with us only what we are. Neither friend or enemy can journey with us. Commendation and condemnation will fall upon ears unheard. Only one word will matter then—His word. Happy shall we be if, out of the shadowy evening of life when our day is full of hush, we hear Him speaking softly, "Well done."

—A. P. Gouthey

AUTHOR BIOGRAPHY

The author of this great work is the Holy Spirit. All praise, honor, and glory goes to Him. I believe that God called me to write to the individual and collective Body of Christ because of the knowledge that I have gained through Christian experience and my many, many years of dedicated service and knowledge gained through reading and studying the bible. Also, I believe that I was chosen because of my willingness to put in the time and the resources necessary to do this kind of work or ministry. It takes time—a lot of time, energy, and money, to do the ministry (writing) that God has called me to do. I am just an instrument that is willing to be used for service.

Inasmuch as the author (Holy Spirit) and the instrument have two different natures, fleshly and divine, there are times that flesh (self) gets in the way of the spirit. In other words, those with the spirit of discernment will be able to discern between the two natures. The Holy Spirit cannot be seen with the natural eye but when and If He is present—a true born again believer will know!

Also, we are all on different levels spiritually, the Bible speaks of "babes" in Christ and a babe in Christ cannot be fed the "meat" of the word. That is process--it takes time! This book, or ministry may not be for you, or you, but it is for someone that the spirit of God is trying to reach and minister to because God's word does not return void.

Many of you know the song, "We are Climbing Jacob's ladder—every round goes higher and higher—Soldiers of the Cross." I am still climbing. My goal and aim however is "higher ground."

Inasmuch as a spirit cannot be seen, I am considered the Author, under the auspices of the Holy Spirit.

Yours in Christ,
The Author, Claudia

www.ingramcontent.com/pod-product-compliance
Lightning Source LLC
Chambersburg PA
CBHW052112070526
44584CB00017B/2447